Real Science-4-Kids

# Teacher's Manual

Level I

Dr. R. W. Keller

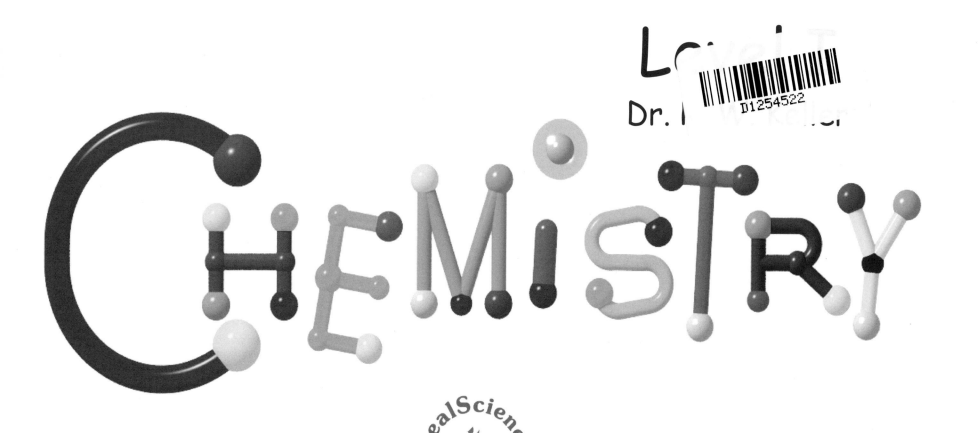

CHEMiSTRY

RealScience
4
Kids

Cover design: David Keller
Opening page: David Keller, Rebecca Keller
Illustrations: Rebecca Keller

**Copyright © 2002, 2005, 2007 Gravitas Publications, Inc.**

Real Science-4-Kids: Chemistry Level I Teacher's Manual


ISBN 10: 0-9749149-8-3
ISBN 13: 9780974914985


Published by Gravitas Publications, Inc.
P.O. Box 4790
Albuquerque, NM 87196-4790


Printed in United States

GRAVITAS
PUBLICATIONS INC

# A note from the author

This curriculum is designed to give students both solid science information and hands-on experimentation. This level is geared towards fourth through sixth grades, but much of the information in the text is very different from what is taught at this grade level in other textbooks. I feel that students beginning in the fourth grade can grasp most of the concepts presented here. This is a *real* science text, so scientific terms are used throughout. It is not important at this time for the students to master the terminology, but it *is* important that they be exposed to the real terms used to describe science.

Each chapter has two parts: a reading part and an experimental part. In the teacher's text, an estimate is given for the time needed to complete each chapter. It is not important that both the reading portion and the experimental portion be conducted in a single sitting. It may be better to split these into two separate days, depending on the interest level of the child and the energy level of the teacher. Also, questions not addressed in the teacher's manual may arise, and extra time may be required to investigate these questions before proceeding with the experimental section.

Each experiment is a *real* science experiment and not just a demonstration. These are designed to engage the students in an actual scientific investigation. The experiments are simple, but they are written the way real scientists actually perform experiments in the laboratory. With this foundation, it is my hope that the students will eventually begin to think of their own experiments and test their own ideas scientifically.

Enjoy!

*R. W. Keller*

# How to use this manual

This teacher's manual provides additional information and answers to the laboratory experiments and review pages for Chemistry, Biology, and Physics. The additional information for each chapter is provided as supplementary material in case questions arise while reading the text. It is not necessary for the students to learn this additional material as most of it is beyond the scope of this level. However, the teacher may find it useful for answering questions.

The laboratory section (or Experiments) together with the Review are found at the end of each chapter. All of the experiments have been tested, but it is not unusual for an experiment to fail. Usually, repeating an experiment helps both student and teacher see where an error may have been made. However, not all repeated experiments work either. Do not worry if an experiment fails. Encourage the student to troubleshoot and investigate possible errors.

# Getting started

The easiest way to follow this curriculum is to have all of the materials needed for each lesson ready before you begin. A small shelf or cupboard or even a plastic bin can be dedicated to holding most of the necessary chemicals and equipment. Those items that need to be fresh are indicated at the beginning of each lesson. The following is a partial list of chemicals and equipment required for the experiments. The items are divided into the following categories; Provided items, Grocery store items, and Speciality store items.

## Provided items
Periodic table of elements (Chemistry Level I text)

## Common household items
paper (white copy paper)

## Grocery store items
several small jars (baby food jars)
two large glass jars (pickle or mayonnaise jar)
white vinegar
balsamic vinegar
baking soda
measuring spoons
eye droppers
Elmer's white glue
Elmer's blue glue
liquid laundry starch (or Borax)
popsicle sticks
distilled water
coffee filters (white)
ammonia
rubbing alcohol
paper towels
bleach
sugar
salt
food coloring
dish soap
wax paper
rubber bands
toothpicks

## Specialty store items

marking pens for writing on glass or wax paper
iodine (Walgreen's or other pharmacy store)
ball point ink pens of various colors (art store)
balance, food scale, mail scale (Office Max)

## Laboratory safety

Most of these experiments use household items. However, some items, such as iodine, are extremely poisonous. Extra care should be taken while working with all chemicals in this series of experiments. The following are some general laboratory precautions that should be applied to the home laboratory:

- Never put things in your mouth unless the experiment tells you to. This means that food items should not be eaten unless it is part of the experiment.

- Use safety glasses while using glass objects or strong chemicals such as bleach.

- Wash hands after handling all chemicals.

- Use adult supervision while working with iodine or glassware and when conductiong any step requiring a stove.

# Contents

CHEMISTRY

# Materials at a glance

| Experiment 1 | Experiment 2 | Experiment 3 | Experiment 4 | Experiment 5 | Experiment 6 | Experiment 7 | Experiment 8 | Experiment 9 | Experiment 10 |
|---|---|---|---|---|---|---|---|---|---|
| pen | toothpicks | baking soda | 1/2 head red cabbage | red cabbage indicator (Exp. 4) | vinegar | multi-colored ink pen | iodine | liquid laundry starch (or Borax) | iodine |
| paper | small marshmallows | lemon juice | distilled water | ammonia | rubbing alcohol | black ink pen | food items: pasta, bread, celery, banana, potato, apple | Elmer's white glue | bread |
| food labels | large marshmallows | balsamic vinegar | small jars | vinegar | ammonia | rubbing alcohol | | Elmer's blue glue | timer |
| dictionary | | sugar | coffee filters | small jars | vegetable oil | coffee filters (white) | | small jars | wax paper |
| encyclopedia | | salt | eye dropper | measuring spoons | melted butter | small jars | liquid laundry starch | marker | marking pen |
| Periodic table of elements | | egg whites (or milk) | ammonia | | small jars | | white paper | popsicle stick for stirring | |
| | | several small jars | vinegar | | food coloring | | eye dropper | | |
| | | eye dropper | soda pop | | dish soap | | | | |
| | | | milk | | | | | | |
| | | | mineral water | | | | | | |

# Chapter 1:  Matter

Time Required:

      Text reading - 30 minutes
      Experimental - 1 hour

Experimental setup:

      NONE

Additional Materials:

      dictionary
      encyclopedia
      food labels

## Overall Objectives:

This chapter will introduce the concept that all things, living and nonliving, are made of the same fundamental components called atoms. It is important to help the students understand that although the world is full of a large number of both living and nonliving things, there is only a limited number of atoms, or elements, that make up all things. The variety observed in all things is a result of the vast number of ways that atoms can be combined with one another. For example, sodium (Na) is found in table salt together with chlorine (Cl) to make "sodium chloride" (NaCl). However, if you add an oxygen atom (O) and make "sodium hypochlorite," NaOCl, you get bleach.

## 1.1 Introduction

*Matter* is a general term for describing what all things are made of.

*Chemistry* is that area of science mainly concerned with the way atoms combine to form chemical bonds.

There are several different subdisciplines within chemistry:

*Physical chemistry* is concerned with the fundamental physics of atoms.

*Biochemistry* is concerned with matter from living things.

*Organic chemistry* is concerned with the chemistry of carbon (C) containing compounds.

*Analytical chemistry* deals with analyzing the composition of matter.

*Inorganic chemistry* is concerned with mostly noncarbon compounds.

## 1.2 Atoms

The students will be introduced to the following terms:

> Atoms
> Protons
> Neutrons
> Electrons

Atoms, protons, neutrons and electrons are more specific terms for matter.

Atoms are very small and cannot be seen by the naked eye. If an atom were the size of a tennis ball, the average man (6 ft. tall) would stand one million kilometers high — almost the distance from here to the sun.

Protons and neutrons are roughly equal in size and both have an atomic mass of 1 amu (atomic mass unit). A proton carries a positive charge and a neutron carries no charge; it is neutral. By comparison, the electron is 1/1836 of the mass of a proton. The electron carries a negative charge that is equal in magnitude to the charge on a proton. For neutral atoms, the number of electrons equals the number of protons. The number of neutrons does not always equal the number of protons or electrons in neutral atoms.

The nucleus contains the protons and neutrons and is much smaller than the full atom. Most of the volume of an atom is occupied by the electrons.

The space occupied by the electrons surrounds the proton-neutron core and is called an orbital or electron cloud. Orbitals can have a variety of shapes, which the students will learn later on. The different shapes of electron clouds are very important for understanding how atoms combine with each other.

## 1.3 Periodic Table

The periodic table of elements is a large chart that organizes and categorizes all of the elements according to their chemical properties.

The periodic table illustrates the general law of periodicity among all of the elements. This means that certain chemical properties of the atoms repeat. For example, fluorine (F) undergoes similar chemical reactions as chlorine (Cl), bromine (Br), iodine (I), and astatine (As). All of these similar elements are arranged in a single column of the periodic table. Grouping the elements according to their chemical properties gives rise to the "periods" which are the horizontal rows.

There are three short periods of 2, 8, and 8 elements:

hydrogen -> helium   [period of 2 elements]
lithium -> neon [period of 8 elements]
sodium -> argon [period of 8 elements]

and then three longer periods of 18, 18, and 32:

potassium -> krypton [period of 18 elements]
rubidium ->xenon [period of 18 elements]
cesium ->radon [period of 32 elements]

The last period is predicted to contain 32 elements, but notice that the number of elements stops at 112.

The last naturally occurring element is uranium at 92 protons. the elements after uranium are artificially made.

The symbols of elements are not always the same as the first letter of the English name since some elements were named in other languages. Some examples are given in the student text.

Page 5 of the student text gives a brief explanation for some of the details in the periodic table.

The number in the upper-left-hand corner of each element square is the atomic number. This number tells how many protons the atom contains. The atomic number is not always in the upper-left-hand corner of the block representing each element: it can be in the middle or on the right.

The number below the name is the atomic weight. The atomic weight is the sum of the weight of the protons, neutrons, and electrons. Because the electrons have essentially no mass, the atomic weight can be considered to be the sum of just the weight for the protons and neutrons. Because protons and neutrons are essentially "1 atomic mass unit" each, the number of neutrons can be determined by subtracting the atomic number from the atomic weight.

Example: Hydrogen has an atomic number of 1. This means that hydrogen has one proton. Hydrogen has an atomic weight close to one, which means that all of the weight is due to the single proton. There are no neutrons.

Another example is uranium:

  number of protons: 92
  atomic weight: 238
  number of neutrons: 238 minus 92 = 146

NOTE:

Although the atomic weight is actually 238.0289, it can be rounded to 238 to calculate the number of neutrons.

Vertically, the elements are organized according to similar chemical properties.

The elements on the far right of the periodic table are the noble gases. The noble gases do not react with other elements in general. It is possible to get some of the noble gases to react, but it is very difficult. The noble gases are always found in nature as single atoms and not in pairs like other gases such as oxygen and nitrogen.

The elements on the far left are called the alkali metals. These elements are very reactive. Lithium (Li), sodium (Na), and potassium (K) react very violently with water. They also form salts with the halogens, which form the column next to the noble gases. Some common salts include sodium chloride (NaCl), lithium chloride (LiCl), potassium chloride (KCl). Sodium chloride (NaCl) is common table salt. Potassium chloride (KCl) is a table salt alternative that is used by many people with high blood pressure.

There are other "trends" or properties that are illustrated with the periodic table, such as atomic size and electronegativity, but these will be introduced later.

The most important points to emphasize with the periodic table are the following:

• All of the elements that make up all things, living and nonliving, are on the periodic table.

• The periodic table illustrates an underlying order or "periodicity" among all of the elements.

• Mendeleev discovered the overall order of elements through scientific investigation and assembled the first periodic table.

## 1.4 Summary

Discuss with the students the main points of this chapter.

- Point out that everything we can touch is made of atoms. Have the students name several different items and discuss how these items are all made of atoms.

- Review that atoms are made of smaller particles called protons, neutrons, and electrons. Protons and neutrons are together in the atomic core, and electrons are found in the electron cloud surrounding the core.

- Review that the number of protons equals the number of electrons in an atom. This is true for neutral atoms. It is possible to remove an electron from an atom or add an electron to an atom. The atom is called an ion in this case. However, this is beyond the scope of this level.

- All of the elements known are found on the periodic table of elements. New elements can be made by man-made means, but all naturally occuring elements are already known.

- Review that all elements are in groups that are similar. For example, the noble gases behave alike and are in the same column.

*NOTES:*

Experiment 1:          What is it made of?          Date:

Objective:

   To become familiar with the periodic table of elements and investigate the composition of some common items.

Materials:
   pen
   paper
   food labels
   dictionary
   encyclopedia
   Periodic Table of Elements

Directions:

1. Take out the periodic table of elements and answer the following questions:
   A. How many protons does aluminum have? How many electrons?
   B. What is the symbol for carbon?
   C. List all of the elements that have chemical properties similar to helium.
   D. What is the atomic weight for nitrogen? How many neutrons does nitrogen have?
2. Next, think of several different items and write them in the column labeled "Item." These can be any item, like "tires" or "cereal." Try to be specific. For example, instead of writing just "cereal," write "corn cereal" or "sweet colored cereal."
3. Next look up in an encyclopedia or on the food label the composition of the items you have selected. Try to be as specific as possible while identifying the composition. For example, if your cereal contains vitamin C, write "sodium ascorbate" if that name is also listed. Try to identify any elements in the compounds you have listed. For example, vitamin C contains the element "sodium."
4. Write the source next to the composition. "Source" means where you got your information, for example, "food label" or "encyclopedia."

The goals of this experiment are to help the students begin to investigate the things in their world and to have them examine what those things are made of.

There are many "right" answers for this experiment, and the elemental composition will not be available for all items from basic resources such as the dictionary or encyclopedia. For example,

Things made of metals:
   soda cans and aluminum foil - aluminum
   silverware (steel) - iron, nickel, silver
   coins - copper, nickel
   jewelry - gold, silver

Things we eat:
   salt - sodium and chlorine
   sugar - carbon, oxygen, hydrogen
   water - hydrogen and oxygen
   bread (carbohydrates) - carbon, oxygen, hydrogen, and other
                              proteins and things.

Also, students can select food items with labels such as cake mixes, cereal, noodles, and vitamins (with vitamins the label is very detailed and the students can also find out how much of something is in the vitamin).

NOTE:
The students DO NOT need to find out every component for each item. To say that cake mix contains salt, flour, and sugar is enough. Let the students go as far as they want with a particular item. Also, it is not necessary to look up components for each item given. Pick a few and go from there.

Sample Answers to Questions:

A. *Aluminum has 13 protons. Aluminum also has 13 electrons.*

B. *The symbol for carbon is "C."*

C. *The elements that have the same chemical properties as helium are neon,*
*argon, krypton xenon, and radon.*

D. *The atomic weight for nitrogen is 14.0067. Nitrogen has 7 neutrons.*

| Item | Composition | Source |
|------|-------------|--------|
| 1. car tires | rubber (carbon and hydrogen) | Webster's Dictionary , page 1582 |
| 2. graham crackers | sodium bicarbonate (sodium) | food label |
| 3. graham crackers | salt (sodium, chlorine) | food label, dictionary, page 1600 |
| 4. | | |
| 5. | | |
| 6. | | |
| 7. | | |
| 8. | | |

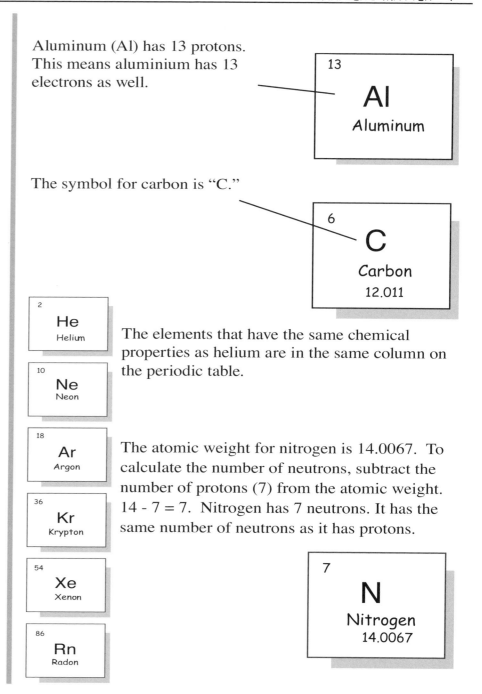

Aluminum (Al) has 13 protons. This means aluminium has 13 electrons as well.

The symbol for carbon is "C."

The elements that have the same chemical properties as helium are in the same column on the periodic table.

The atomic weight for nitrogen is 14.0067. To calculate the number of neutrons, subtract the number of protons (7) from the atomic weight. 14 - 7 = 7. Nitrogen has 7 neutrons. It has the same number of neutrons as it has protons.

## Results:

Briefly describe what you discovered about the composition of the various items.

For example,

Kellogg's Sugar Smacks™ cereal contains vitamin C which is called sodium ascorbate.

*Table salt is made of sodium and chlorine.*

*Iodized table salt contains sodium, chlorine, and iodine.*

*Chocolate cake mix contains sugar.*

*Sugar has oxygen, hydrogen ,and carbon in it.*

## Conclusions:

State here what "conclusions" can be made.

For example,

Many cereals contain sodium in the form of salt and vitamin C.

*Some peanut butter contains sugar.*

*Rubber contains  carbon and hydrogen.*

Help the students write accurate statements about the data they have collected.

Some examples are given.

Help the students think specifically about what their data show. This is an important critical thinking step that will help them evaluate future experiments.

Try to help them write concluding statements that are valid. Encourage them to avoid stating options or anything that cannot be drawn strictly from their data.

For example, it may be true that all cereals contain "salt." However, this particular investigation cannot confirm or deny that conclusion. The most that can be stated from this investigation is "Brand X contains salt, and Brand Y contains salt" but any further statement is conjecture.

Help them formulate their conclusions using the words *some*, *all*, *many*, and *none*. Point out that the statement, "All cereals contain salt" is not valid, but based on this investigation it is valid to say, "Some cereals contain salt."

Again, there are numerous "right" answers. One student may list "sugar" as a component in soup, and another may list "salt," and both could be "right." The true test is whetether the statements about the data are valid or not valid.

Also, try to show them where broad statements can be made accordingly. For example, "All U.S. pennies contain copper" is probably a valid statement even though we haven't checked every U.S. penny.

This may seem fairly subtle, but the main point is to help them understand the kinds of valid conclusions science can offer based on scientific investigation.

## Review

Define the following terms:

chemistry     *A branch of science concerned with the properties of matter.*

matter     *A general term for what makes up all things.*

atoms (*atomos*) *The fundamental building blocks of matter. Atomos is a Greek word that means uncuttable.*

proton     *A small particle found inside atoms.*

neutron     *Another small particle found inside atoms.*

electron     *A particle found in an atom that is very much smaller than both protons and neutrons.*

nucleus     *The central portion of an atom that consists of only the protons and neutrons.*

electron cloud *The space occupied by the electrons surrounding the nucleus.*

element     *Another name for any of the distinct atoms in the periodic table.*

atomic weight *The total weight of an atom; the weight of the protons and neutrons combined.*

# Chapter 2: Molecules

Time Required:

> Text reading - 1 hour
> Experimental - 1 hour

Experimental setup:

> NONE

Additional Materials:

> Small marshmallows
> Large marshmallows

## Overall Objectives:

In this chapter the students will explore how atoms combine to make molecules. They will discover that in order to make molecules the atoms must obey certain rules. These rules control how the atoms combine.

## 2.1 From atoms to molecules

Atoms combine with other atoms to make molecules. The connection between two atoms is called a bond. The specifics of bonding are quite complicated and beyond the scope of this level, so many of the more complicated details will not be discussed. However, some of the general concepts will be introduced.

## 2.2  Forming bonds

Bonds are formed via the electrons in an atom. When two atoms combine, the spaces surrounding each central core (the electron orbitals) merge. The electrons of each atom share this combined space. The electrons themselves are not always evenly distributed within this space (see Section 2.5), but the space that each electron occupied on a single atom is now combined with the space of the other atom.

The ability of an atom to form a bond with another atom depends on whether or not its electron cloud has enough "space" to accommodate new electrons. For example, the electron orbital of a hydrogen atom can accommodate a total of two electrons. Because a single hydrogen atom has only one electron, it can bond with another hydrogen atom that has one electron to make a molecule such that their combined electron cloud has two electrons.  The electron orbitals for both of the hydrogen

atoms become full, and a hydrogen molecule cannot bond with any other atom.  Compare this to a helium atom.  Helium is a noble gas and cannot bond with any other atom.  Why?  Because it already has two electrons in its orbital and there is no space available to accommodate additional electrons.  All of the noble gases have "full" orbitals.  This is the reason they don't easily bond to other atoms.

## 2.3 Types of bonds

The two general types of bonds that atoms make are as follows:

1. Shared electron bonds, or covalent bonds

2. Unshared electron bonds, or ionic bonds.

The terms "shared" and "unshared" are descriptive terms used to describe the two general types of bonds: covalent and ionic. Covalent bonds are those bonds made by atoms that mostly share their electrons. Ionic bonds form when one atom "gives up" an electron to another atom and the electrons are essentially unshared.

## 2.4 Shared electron bonds

Atoms that are identical always make covalent bonds.  For example the bond between two hydrogen atoms is covalent, the bond between two carbon atoms is covalent, and the bond between two oxygen atoms is covalent.  These atoms form covalent bonds because both of the atoms, being identical, will have the same ability to give away or to receive electrons.  Covalent bonds between two identical atoms are "pure" covalent bonds, which means there is equal sharing.

Covalent bonds can also be formed between two atoms that are not alike but that have a similar ability to pull away or give electrons. Oxygen and carbon, for example, form covalent bonds. These bonds are not "pure" covalent bonds. In fact, their electrons are not entirely equally shared since oxygen has a slightly higher tendency to keep more electrons for itself. However, they are still considered to form a covalent bond because the electrons are mostly shared.

## 2.5 Unshared electron bonds

When atoms do not share electrons, they form ionic bonds. In this case the electrons are almost exclusively on one or the other atom and are not equally shared, or even slightly shared. When an atom has more or fewer electrons than it would normally have, it is called an ion. In a molecule with unequally shared electrons, one atom will have more electrons than it should, and the other atom will have fewer electrons. Each atom is called an ion. The bond is called an ionic bond.

When sodium and chlorine combine, they form an ionic bond, because the electrons are not shared equally. The chlorine wants all of the electrons for itself, and the sodium is willing to give up its electron and just hang out next to the chlorine.

## 2.6 Bonding rules

The number of bonds and the type of bonds an atom will form depend on the number of electrons available and the type of atoms forming the bonds.

The maximum number of bonds an element can form depends on the number of available electrons. *Available* is emphasized because although an element may have 53 electrons, it cannot form 53 bonds. To form a bond, it takes two electrons, one from each atom. The electron that forms a bond must be available and cannot be part of a full orbital. For example, the element iodine has 53 electrons, but it has only one free electron. The other 52 are not available because they are in filled shells.

At this point, understanding how many electrons make how many bonds and which kind is not important, the main point is the following:

*Atoms follow rules to form bonds with other atoms.*

Here are a few atoms with the number of bonds they typically form:

Hydrogen : 1
Sodium: 1
Beryllium: 2
Boron: 3
Carbon: 4
Nitrogen: 3
Oxygen: 2
Fluorine: 1

Also, though this is not mentioned in the text, some atoms can form double or triple bond. For example, carbon dioxide, $CO_2$, has two double bonds between carbon and oxygen: O=C=O. Carbon still has 4 bonds and oxygen still has two bonds, but carbon is not bonded to 4 different atoms.

## 2.7 Shapes of molecules

The molecules that result when two or more atoms combine also have particular shapes. The shapes depend on the number of electrons for each atom and the type of bond they form. Again, the details of how molecules are shaped are not important. The point is,

*The shapes of molecules also obey rules.*

Some common shapes include:

Carbon with four single bonds:  tetrahedral

Carbon with two double bonds: linear

Boron with three single bonds:  trigonal planar

Nitrogen with three single bonds: pyramidal

side view        top view

## 2.8 Summary

Discuss with the students the following main points of this chapter:

• Atoms combine with other atoms to make molecules.

• The connections between atoms in a molecule are called bonds. There are two types of bonds: covalent and ionic.

• Atoms follow rules when they form bonds. The number of bonds an atom can form depends on the number of available electrons on the atom.

• The shapes of molecules also follow rules, and molecules have certain shapes.

Experiment 2:     Making marshmallow molecules     Date:

Objective:
   To learn how atoms fit together by making marshmallow molecules.

Materials:
   small colored marshmallows
   large marshmallows
   toothpicks

Experiment:

1. Take several marshmallows of both sizes and several toothpicks.

2. Make shapes from the marshmallows and toothpicks.  First, form any number of links between marshmallows - i.e. put any number of toothpicks into each marshmallow.  Draw the shapes below, noting the number of toothpicks in each marshmallow.

*Not following any rules.*

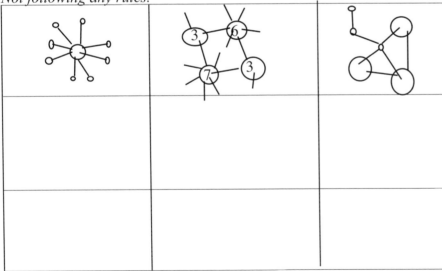

In this experiment the students will use marshmallows to explore how atoms fit together to make molecules.

Have the students record the date on the top line.

Discuss the objective.

Materials:

   The materials for this experiment are marshmallows and toothpicks.

   Two sizes of marshmallows are preferred, but one size will work.

   Gum drops or jellybeans can also be used.

Experiment:

First, have the students make marshmallow molecules without any rules.  Encourage the students to make molecules of various sizes and shapes.  They do not need to record every shape they make, but try to get them to draw as many different shapes as they can.

Some suggested shapes are shown on the left.

There are no "wrong" answers as all shapes are valid in this step.

3. Now assign an "atom" to each of the marshmallows.  The large marshmallows should be C, N, and O and the small marshmallows should be H and Cl.  Use the following "rules" for the number of toothpicks that can go into a marshmallow.

Carbon - 4 toothpicks all pointing away from each other

Nitrogen - 3 toothpicks pointing downward

Oxygen - 2 toothpicks pointing downward

Hydrogen and Chlorine - 1 toothpick pointing in any direction.

Cl or H

4. Next, try to make the following molecules from your marshmallow atoms:

H$_2$O :  This is one oxygen and two hydrogens.
Follow the rules above, and draw the shape on the following chart:.

NH$_3$:  This is one nitrogen and three hydrogens.
Follow the rules above, and draw the shape on the following chart:.

CH4:  This is one carbon and four hydrogens
Follow the rules above, and draw the shape on the following chart:.

CH$_3$OH:  This is one carbon with three hydrogens and one oxygen attached.  The oxygen has one hydrogen.
Follow the rules above, and draw the shape on the following chart:.

Next, the students will make "real" molecule models following specific rules.

The rules for carbon, nitrogen, oxygen, hydrogen and chlorine are shown.  Note that the orientation of the bonds (toothpicks) are also important. The students can first try to put the toothpicks into several marshmallows following these rules before making molecules.
Note that the large marshmallows are assigned to carbon, nitrogen and oxygen.  If this is confusing, try to differentiate between the molecules by adding a drop of food coloring to each.

Next, the students will make "molecules" with the marshmallow "atoms."  Some molecules are given as examples.

The names of these molecules are as follows:

H$_2$O : water

NH$_3$: ammonia

CH$_4$: methane

CH$_3$OH:  methanol

CCl$_4$: four chlorine atoms with one central carbon (carbon tetrachloride)

CH$_3$CH$_3$: two carbon atoms connected with three hydrogens each (ethane)

CH$_2$Cl$_2$:  two hydrogen atoms and two chlorine atoms all connected to one central carbon atom (dichloromethane).

The correct shapes for the example molecules are displayed on the left.

Have the students note the number of bonds for each molecule and ask them whether or not they followed the rules.

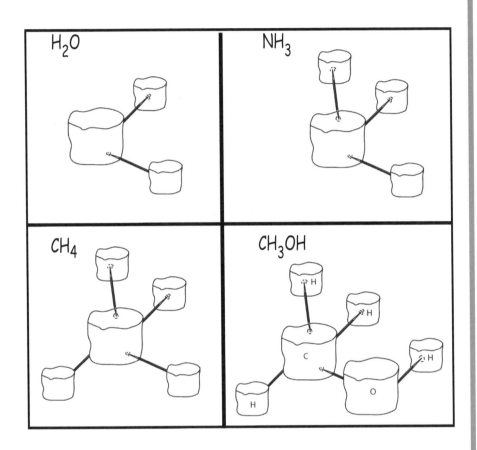

5. Now following the "rules" outlined in step 3 for the marshmallow molecules, make other "molecules." Make as many different shapes as you can without breaking the "rules." Draw your shapes in the boxes below.

Next, the students will follow the rules and make their own "molecules." Have them note how many bonds each "atom" forms.

Some suggested molecules are the following:

$CCl_4$ : four chlorine atoms with one central carbon (carbon tetrachloride)

$CH_3CH_3$: two carbon atoms connected with three hydrogens each (ethane)

$CH_3CH_2OH$ : two carbon atoms with two toothpicks between them, each with two hydrogens. This also obeys the rules (ethanol).

The students can build many different molecules.

## Conclusions:

*Many different shapes can be made without following the rules.*

*The large marshmallows can hold up to twenty toothpicks with no rules.*

*I could only find five shapes (following the rules).*

Have the students write some conclusions about the molecules they have created with their marshmallows.

Sample conlusions are given, but these are only examples and not necessarily the conclusions they will find. Help them try to be specific with the conclusions they write.

Emphasize the fact that there should be fewer molecules possible when the atoms obey the rules. "Fewer possible molecules" means that there is not a random arrangement of molecules that make up the world. Atoms have special properties that result in molecules with special properties. Molecules with special properties mean that higher structures, such as tissues, plants, stars, jellyfish, and pudding, also have special properties.

Review

Define the following terms:

molecule   *When two or more atoms are combined.*

bond        *The connection between two atoms.*

ionic bond        *A bond with unshared electrons*

covalent bond    *A bond with shared electrons.*

sodium chloride        *A molecule made by combining sodium and chlorine (also known as table salt).*

Answer the following questions:

How many bonds does hydrogen typically form?   *One*

How many bonds does carbon typically form?        *Four*

How many bonds does nitrogen typically form?      *Three*

How many bonds does oxygen typically form?        *Two*

Draw the shape of water:

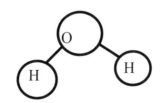

*NOTES:*

# Chapter 3: Chemical Reactions

Time Required:

Text reading - 1 hour
Experimental - 1 hour

Experimental setup:

NONE

Additional Materials:

Lemon juice
Balsamic vinegar
Egg whites
Baking soda
Milk
Sugar
Salt

*Overall Objectives:*

In this chapter the students will begin to learn how atoms and molecules react to form and break chemical bonds. It is not important for the students to memorize the names of the reactions. Help them understand that in chemical reactions, the atoms are rearranged. The protons and neutrons are not being changed.

## 3.1 Introduction

Point out to the students that chemical reactions occur everywhere.

For example:

*Stomach acid digests our food.*

*When hair is straightened or permed, sulfur bonds are broken and reformed.*

*Cars are powered by the combustion (chemical reaction) of gasoline with oxygen in the air.*

*When iron is left outside, it reacts with oxygen and rust forms.*

Four main divisions of chemical reactions are given. These are called *combination reactions, decomposition reactions, displacement reactions,* and *exchange reactions*. Most chemical reactions fall into these categories or are combinations of these categories.

## 3.2 Combination reaction

In a combination reaction, two or more molecules combine to form a single product. The example shown is the formation of sodium chloride by combining sodium metal and chlorine gas.

NOTE:
In the reaction between sodium metal and chlorine gas, the chlorine gas is a dimer (two atoms of chlorine). The bond between the chlorine atoms is broken before the formation of sodium chloride, so there is an extra step that is not shown.

## 3.3 Decomposition reaction

In a decomposition reaction, molecules decompose or "break down" to form other molecules.

Note that two molecules of water decompose into one molecule of oxygen gas and two molecules of hydrogen gas. This is called a balanced reaction because the number of H and O atoms is the same on both sides; only the nature of the bond changes.

## 3.4 Displacement reaction

A displacement reaction is slightly harder to visualize than the other two reactions because bonds are breaking and reforming at once. In the reaction of water with sodium metal, the sodium atoms displace a hydrogen atom on each of the water molecules. The two free hydrogens then combine to make hydrogen gas ($H_2$).

Again note that the reaction is balanced in that two water molecules are shown reacting with two sodium atoms giving two molecules of sodium hydroxide and one molecule of hydrogen gas.

## 3.5 Exchange reaction

In an exchange reaction, the atoms trade places. The example shown is the reaction of hydrochloric acid (HCl) and sodium hydroxide (NaOH). Again, bonds are both breaking and forming in this reaction.

This particular exchange reaction is also an acid-base reaction and will be covered in more detail in subsequent chapters. Hydrochloric acid is a very strong acid and very harmful if swallowed. Sodium hydroxide is a very strong base and also very harmful if swallowed. Both of these will also cause burns on skin. However, when they are added together and react, they make table salt (which we eat) and water. If concentrated reagents are used, the reaction is quite violent and will produce a large amount of heat.

## 3.6 Spontaneous or not?

Not all reactions occur spontaneously. Some reactions, like the decomposition of water, require energy input before the reaction will proceed. The reasons why one reaction is spontaneous and another is not are beyond the scope of this level. The key concepts are "enthalpy" and "entropy." These are described in a branch of chemistry called chemical thermodynamics.

## 3.7 Evidences for chemical reactions

There are several indicators that tell scientists when a chemical reaction has taken place. These include bubbles, color change, heat exchange, and precipitation. Sometimes more than one of these can occur at the same time. Both bubbles and heat can be given off together. Sometimes none of them occur and more subtle methods must be used to detect the reaction.

Bubbles form when one of the molecules produced is a gas.

Color changes may indicate a variety of end products. Compounds that contain metals, like copper (Cu), often display color. Blood, for example, contains iron (Fe). When blood is combined with oxygen it is bright red; however, without oxygen it is a darker red.

A solution can either give off heat (exothermic) or take in heat (endothermic). Most exothermic reactions are spontaneous.

Precipitations occur when one or more products of the reaction are no longer soluble in the solution.

## 3.8 Summary

Discuss with the students the following main points of this chapter:

• Molecules and atoms react with each other to form new molecules.

• There are four basic types of chemical reactions, and these can combine for more complicated reactions.

• Not all reactions occur spontaneously.

• Some chemical reactions can be observed.

Experiment 3:      Identifying Chemical Reactions     Date: _____

Objective:

In this experiment we will try to identify a chemical reaction by observing the changes that occur when two solutions are added together.

Hypothesis:

A chemical reaction can be identified by observing changes that occur in the course of the reaction.

Materials:
baking soda
lemon juice
balsamic vinegar
sugar (1-2 Tbs dissolved in 1/2 cup of water)
salt (1-2 Tbs dissolved in 1/2 cup of water)
egg whites
milk
several small jars
eye dropper

Experiment:

1.  Look at the chart in the Results section.  Write down all of the items (i.e. baking soda, lemon juice, balsamic vinegar, sugar, salt, and egg whites) horizontally  above the boxes of each column.

2.  Now write the same list of items vertically down the left side of the grid, next to the boxes for each row.

3.  There should be an item assigned to each column and to each row.

4.  In the boxes in the middle, record what you observe when the item listed in the column is mixed with the item in the corresponding row.

In this experiment the students will examine chemical reactions and try to identify when they happen.

Select a variety of food items.  Bleach and ammonia cause good chemical reactions, but they can give off strong odors and this combination is not recommended.

Have the students put a small amount of each item into a jar.

Have the students examine the contents of each jar.

Note the color and odor wherever possible.

Although most of the items are food items, do not allow the students to taste them.

Have the students record the color, texture, and odor next to each item in the materials list wherever possible.

For example:

Baking Soda:   white powder, no odor
Balsamic Vinegar:  dark liquid, sour odor

5. Look especially for changes that indicate a chemical reaction has taken place. For example, look for bubbles, color change, or a precipitate.

6. Ask your teacher for the unknown solutions. When you mix them try to determine whether a chemical reaction has taken place. Try to identify what the unknown solutions are.

Results:

| | milk | lemon juice | salt water | baking soda | vinegar | egg whites |
|---|---|---|---|---|---|---|
| milk | | REACT *precipitate* | NO | NO | REACT *precipitate* | NO |
| lemon juice | REACT *precipitate* | | NO | REACT *bubbles* | NO | REACT *precipitate* |
| salt water | NO | NO | | NO | NO | NO |
| baking soda | NO | REACT *bubbles* | NO | | REACT *bubbles* | NO |
| vinegar | REACT *precipitate* | NO | NO | REACT *bubbles* | | REACT *precipitate* |
| egg whites | NO | REACT *precipitate* | NO | NO | REACT *precipitate* | |

Have the students write the "reagents" on the top and side of the grid. The bottom boxes can be marked out, or each reaction can be performed twice. It might be nice to check the order of addition; add lemon juice to baking soda, then add baking soda to lemon juice, to see if a difference can be observed (the order of addition should not matter). This is optional.

Have the students record their observations in the boxes for each reaction.

JUST FOR FUN:

Watch baking soda decompose and give off carbon dioxide gas while making peanut brittle.

### Peanut Brittle

1 1/2 cups sugar
1 cup syrup (white Karo)
1/2 cup water

1 1/2 cups raw peanuts
1 teaspoon soda
buttered pan

Boil sugar, water and syrup in a sauce pan on medium heat until it turns a little brown. Add 1 1/2 cups raw peanuts. Stir until golden brown. Don't over brown. Add 1 teaspoon soda. Spread in buttered pan.

Unknowns:

Descriptions

1._____

2._____

Result when the two are mixed:_____

What could they be?_____

Conclusions:

_____

_____

_____

_____

_____

_____

Give the students two "unknowns." These can either be two that will react or two that won't react. It can be done more than once. The students may want to give you an "unknown" to see if you can identify it.

Explain to the students that much of the time scientists are trying to figure out how to identify unknowns. The students have observed all of the reactants both before and after a reaction. They now have the necessary knowledge to identify an unknown.

Another option is to give the students only one unknown. Have them guess what it might be before performing any tests. Then have the student test this unknown with each of the other reactants. Have them prove the identity of the unknown with the chemical reactions they have already observed.

Have the students write valid conclusions. Help them state conclusions that reflect only the data found in this experiment. For example, "Salt water does not react with anything" is not a valid conclusion because we haven't tested everything. However, "Salt water does not react with any of the items we tested" is valid.

## Review

What are the four types of chemical reactions?

*decomposition reaction*
*combination reaction*
*displacement reaction*
*exchange reaction*

Define the following terms:

chemical reaction    *A process where chemical bonds are broken or created between atoms and molecules.*

combination reaction    *A reaction in which two molecules combine to form a single product.*

decomposition reaction    *A reaction in which a molecule breaks apart to make two or more new molecules*

displacement reaction    *A reaction in which one atom releases another atom from a molecule.*

exchange reaction    *A reaction in which one atom trades places with another atom on a different molecule.*

spontaneous    *Term describing when a reaction happens automatically.*

List four changes that can be observed when a chemical reaction has taken place.

*bubbles forming*
*color change*
*temperature change*
*precipitate formation*

*NOTES:*

# Chapter 4:  Acids, Bases, and pH

Time Required:

    Text reading - 30 minutes
    Experimental - 1 hour
    Experimental setup: 0.5 hours

Experimental setup:

    cooking pot for boiling water

Additional Materials:

    One head of red cabbage
    Distilled water
    The following solutions:
        Ammonia
        Mineral water
        Vinegar
        Soda pop
        Milk

## Overall Objectives:

This chapter introduces acids, bases, pH and pH indicators. It is not important that the students understand the details of an acid-base reaction. This chapter will serve as an introduction to the overall concepts and terminology.

## 4.1 Introduction

An acid-base reaction is a type of exchange reaction. In the example on page 21, the hydrogen atom from acetic acid trades places with the sodium atom from sodium bicarbonate. Explain to the student that vinegar is a type of acid, called acetic acid, and baking soda is a type of base. The formal name for baking soda is *sodium bicarbonate*.

Discuss with the students which atoms change places. Show them from the drawing that hydrogen exchanges places with sodium. Explain that the other atoms remain the same.

NOTE:

The molecules are not drawn with the bonds showing, and on first inspection it appears that the central carbon on both molecules has broken the rule of "4 bonds for carbon." Also, two of the oxygens appear to have broken the rule for "2 bonds for oxygen." However, in each case the bond between the central carbon atom and one of the oxygen atoms is a double bond. Double bonds are beyond the scope of the this level, but all of the bonding rules are satisfied.

## 4.2 The pH scale

The pH scale is important, but mathematically and conceptually the actual definition of pH is too difficult for this level. pH is pronounced by just saying the letters "P" and "H." pH is actually a measure of the hydrogen ion concentration (written as [H]). The mathematical expression for pH is:

$$pH = -\log [H]$$

The higher the hydrogen ion concentration, the lower the pH, the lower the hydrogen ion concentration, the higher the pH. The hydrogen ion concentration is the real definition of what is meant by "acid" in this chapter.

The chart on page 22 of the student text shows the pH for various solutions. Discuss the chart with the students. Show them that many of the foods we eat are near neutral pH. Show them that some foods are acidic, like vinegar. Explain to the students that this is why vinegar has a very strong sour taste.

Discuss with the students some other items and their pH. For example, explain that both oranges and lemons are acidic, but the medicine used to treat an upset stomach is basic.

Other items not on the chart:

Lemons - pH 2.4

Oranges - pH 3.4

Seawater - pH 8.5 to 10

Milk of magnesia - pH 10.5

## 4.3  Properties of acids and bases

The properties of acids and bases are quite different, and in many ways opposite.

*Acids are sour, not slippery, and effective in dissolving metals.*

*Bases are bitter, slippery, and reactive with metals to form precipitates.*

Students should NOT taste solutions to determine if they are acids or bases. Before modern techniques were available, many chemists tasted things to find out more about them. However, this is quite dangerous, and today scientists do not taste anything in the laboratory.

If the students want to test the slipperiness of a solution, a household cleaner like ammonia can be diluted 1:10 and they can feel the difference between this and vinegar. Proton concentration (or pH) is the real definition of what we mean by "acid" in this chapter.

## 4.4  Measuring pH

Scientists measure pH with pH meters, pH paper, or solution indicators.

The most common laboratory technique for measuring pH is to use a pH meter. There are a variety of pH meters and electrodes available. The most common electrode is called a glass electrode. There is a small glass ball at the end of this electrode that senses the pH electrically.

Before pH meters, pH paper was the most common way to measure pH. Litmus paper can still be found in most laboratories together with other types of pH paper. There are two types of litmus paper. The blue litmus tests for acidic solutions and the red tests for basic solutions. Litmus paper is not suitable for determining the exact pH; it can only indicate if a solution is acidic or basic. Other types of pH paper can more accurately determine the actual pH.

Litmus paper is made with a compound called an indicator. An indicator is any molecule that changes colors as a result of a pH change.

The table gives some common indicators used in the laboratory. Some of these are difficult to pronounce, but many can be looked up in a dictionary or encyclopedia for pronunciation guidance.

The chart on page 24 of the student text is meant to illustrate that there are a variety of pH indicators that can be used over a wide range of pH. Often pH indicators are mixed so that more than one pH range can be detected.

## 4.5  Summary

Discuss the following main points of this chapter with the students:

- An acid-base reaction is a special kind of exchange reaction. Have the students look again at the illustration in section 4.1 and discuss how the atoms on each molecule trade places.

- pH measures the acidity or basicity of a solution. Have the students look again at the pH of a base, the pH of an acid, and the pH of a neutral solution.

- Review the various methods for measuring pH; pH paper, pH meters, and pH indicators.

*NOTES:*

Experiment 4:    Making an acid-base indicator    Date: _____

Objective:  _We will make an acid-base indicator from red cabbage and use it_
            _to determine which solutions are acidic or basic._

Hypothesis:  _We can use an indicator to identify acidic or basic solutions._
_____

Materials:

    half a head of red cabbage
    distilled water
    small jars
    coffee filters
    eye dropper
    various solutions: for example,
      ammonia
      mineral water
      vinegar
      soda pop
      milk

Experiment:

1. Take half of the head of red cabbage and divide it into several pieces.

2. Place three cups of distilled water in a pan, and bring the water to a boil.

3. Place the cabbage in the boiling water and boil for several minutes.

4. Remove the cabbage and let the water cool.  The water should be a deep purple color.

5. Take one cup of the cabbage water for this experiment and REFRIGERATE the rest for the next experiment.

6. Cut the coffee filters into small strips, about 2 cm wide and 4 cm long. Make at least 20.

Have the students write their own objective and hypothesis for this experiment.  Some examples are given.

The following list of items is recommended:

    ammonia
    mineral water
    vinegar
    soda pop
    milk

These are both acids and bases and milk is neutral.

Other suggested items include:

    water (neutral)
    Windex or other glass cleaner (basic)
    Lemon juice, or orange juice (acidic)
    White grape juice (acidic)

The cabbage water produces enough material for this experiment and the one in Chapter 5.  It is important to refrigerate the cabbage juice, or it will spoil and cannot be used for the next experiment.  It should keep about two weeks in the refrigerator.

Make 20 or more paper strips in case more solutions will be tested. The cabbage indicator can be added to the strips of paper several times and dried in between.  This makes the color change more dramatic.

7. With the eye dropper, put several drops of the cabbage mixture onto the filter papers and allow them to dry. They should be slightly pink and uniform in color. If the papers are too light, more solution can be dropped onto them and then they can be dried again. This is your acid indicator paper.

8. Label one of the jars "Control Acid" and place a tablespoon of vinegar into the jar. Add 5 tablespoons of water. This is your *known* acid.

9. Label another jar "Control Base" and add a tablespoon of ammonia to the jar. Add 5 tablespoons of water. This is your *known* base.

10. Put one tablespoon of the other solutions you have collected into separate jars and add 2 to 5 tablespoons of water to each.

11. Carefully dip the pH paper into the "Control Acid" and record your results. Look immediately at the paper for a color change. Tape the paper in the book under "Control Acid."

12. Carefully dip a new piece of pH paper into the "Control Base" and record your results. Look immediately for a color change. Tape the paper in the book under "Control Base."

13. Now take new pH paper and dip it into the other solutions you have made. Record your results. Tape the papers into the book.

Results:

| Item | color of pH paper | Acid/Base? | Notes |
|---|---|---|---|
| Control Acid | pink | acid | |
| Control Base | green | base | |
| | | | |
| | | | |
| | | | |
| | | | |
| | | | |
| | | | |

In this experiment the students are introduced to "controls." A control is an experiment where the outcome is already known, or where a given outcome can be determined. The control provides a point of reference or comparison for the experiments using unknowns. For example, in this experiment the students will test for acidity or basicity with a pH indicator, but they do not know what the expected color change will be. By doing controls, with solutions that they know are either acidic (vinegar) or basic (ammonia), they can determine what the color change for an acid is and what the color change for a base is. Only then can they test for the "unknown" solutions.

Control experiments also tell the scientist when the experiment has failed. If no color change is observed with a control, something is wrong with the setup or design of the experiment. Control experiments help scientists check for errors.

The ammonia (control base) should turn the paper green.
The vinegar (control acid) should turn the paper pink.

The color change observed on the pH paper may be quick or it may be subtle. It is best to look at the paper immediately after it has been dipped into the solution. If it is too difficult to determine what the color change on the paper is, the cabbage indicator can be used directly. Simply pour a small amount (a teaspoon or two) into the solution directly and record the color change.

| Item | color of pH paper | Acid/Base? | Notes |
|------|-------------------|------------|-------|
|      |                   |            |       |
|      |                   |            |       |
|      |                   |            |       |
|      |                   |            |       |
|      |                   |            |       |
|      |                   |            |       |
|      |                   |            |       |
|      |                   |            |       |
|      |                   |            |       |
|      |                   |            |       |
|      |                   |            |       |
|      |                   |            |       |
|      |                   |            |       |
|      |                   |            |       |

Help the students be specific and make valid conclusions from their data. If something did not change color, but the experimental controls worked, it is probably true that the solution is neutral or near neutral. However, if no color change is observed or if the result is ambiguous, it may not be true that the solution is neutral, or it may be that it is just difficult to tell.

Have the students draw conclusions even if they experienced difficulties.

**Conclusions:** *(The following are examples of valid conclusions.)*

*Ammonia is basic.  Basic solutions turn green with the cabbage indicator.*

*Vinegar is acidic.  Acidic solutions turn pink with the cabbage indicator.*

*Grape juice turned the paper purple.  Because grape juice is already purple,*

*it cannot be concluded from this experiment if grape juice is acidic, basic, or*

*neutral.*

## Review

Define the following terms:

electrode     *The part of the pH meter that goes directly into the solution that detects the pH of the solution.*

pH meter     *An instrument that measures pH.*

litmus paper     *A special paper that can be used to measure pH.*

acid-base indicator   *Any solution that changes color as a result of pH.*

acid-base reaction   *A special type of exchange reaction between and acid and a base.*

control   *A reaction, or test ,whose outcome is already known.*

Answer the following questions:

What is the pH of a neutral solution?   *seven*

What is the pH of an acidic solution?   *less than seven*

What is the pH of a basic solution?   *more than seven*

Is vinegar an acid or a base?   *Vinegar is an acid.*

Is baking soda an acid or a base?   *A solution of baking soda is basic.*

What is the chemical name for vinegar?  *acetic acid*

What is the chemical name for baking soda?   *sodium bicarbonate*

*NOTES:*

# Chapter 5:  Acid-Base Neutralization

Time Required:

  Text reading - 1 hour
  Experimental - 30 minutes

Experimental setup:

  Acid-base indicator made in
  Experiment 4

Additional Materials:

  Ammonia
  Vinegar

## Overall Objectives:

In this chapter the students will be introduced to additional details about the acid-base reaction of vinegar and baking soda. The students will also be given a chance to plot data and perform an acid-base titration in the experimental section of this chapter.

## 5.1 Introduction

On page 26 of the student text the overall reaction for acetic acid (vinegar) and sodium bicarbonate (baking soda) is shown. Have the students look carefully at the drawing and note the various steps.

The main points to emphasize on this page are as follows:

- Acids and bases neutralize each other to make "salt" and water.

- This particular acid-base reaction (vinegar and baking soda) is actually TWO reactions; an exchange reaction and a decomposition reaction. (See Chapter 3.)

- The pH of the final solution is 7 (neutral) if equal concentrations and amounts of acid and base are combined.

The decomposition portion of the reaction is marked in the gray dotted box. The bubbles that are released from the reaction are carbon dioxide, $(CO_2)$, and the solution that remains is water and sodium acetate, a salt. Sodium acetate is NOT the same as table salt.

## 5.2 Concentration

Here the students will be introduced to concentration.

The concentration of something is simply the number of molecules in a given volume. A bottle of concentrated hand soap, for example, has more soap molecules (or less water) in it than one that is not concentrated. Because it is more concentrated, it takes less soap to make a lather than a less concentrated product; but it is still the same soap.

The same is true for acids and bases. If a solution is concentrated, it has more molecules in it that make it either acidic or basic. Therefore it is stronger.

This is illustrated with the difference between glacial acetic acid (concentrated acetic acid) and vinegar (dilute acetic acid). Glacial acetic acid has a very pungent odor and will burn skin on contact. Vinegar is the same acid, but much less concentrated and safe to eat.

The neutralization process of acids and bases are used in everyday life. Antacids are bases that are used to neutralized the hydrochloric acid in the stomach.

## 5.3 Titration

On page 28 of the student text the students are introduced to titrations. A titration is a technique where one substance is added to another substance in small quantities. By adding the second substance in small quantities, any small change in the solution conditions, or other properties, can be observed. The technique of titration is used not only for acid-base reactions and other reactions as well.

For an acid-base reaction, the concentration of an unknown acid or base can be determined by doing a titration. How does this work? Acids and bases neutralize each other. If you start with an acid solution and add a base, the base will neutralized the acid. Once all of the acid has been neutralized the next drop of base will cause teh pH to change dramatically. If the concentration of one solution (acid or base) is known, then the concentration of the other unknown solution can be determined.

It is not important that the students fully grasp this concept. It is enough for them to know that an acid and a base will neutralize each other. An example of plotting data is given since plotting will be used in the experimental section of this chapter.

## 5.4 Plotting data

Organizing data into plots, charts, and diagrams is very important for understanding data. It is a basic scientific skill, and students should be able to organize and plot data.

There are many different ways to plot data. The example given on page 29 of the student text is a simple line plot. A bar graph could also work for this illustration. Another type of plot is a pie chart. All of these are used to illustrate data in a way that makes it easier to understand.

In this example the height and age of several people are collected. The data are shown in the small table above the plot. Show the students that it is difficult to tell the connection between age and height just by *looking* at the data in the table. Also, point out that if more data were collected, say over 100 people, it would be very difficult to tell what the data show.

Next discuss the plot at the bottom of the page. Tell the students that the plot is a way to visualize the data to make it easier to understand. The two axes are height and age. Show them that for every person a height and age are given and that these two data values intersect at a point on the plot. In this way all of the data from the table can be transferred to the plot.

Discuss how a line can be drawn to connect the points on the plot and this line helps show that as age goes up, height goes up only to a point and does not continue like age, but instead height levels off.

## 5.5 Plot of an acid-base titration

On page 30 of the student text is a typical plot of an acid-base titration. In this plot the base is added to a fixed volume of acid. Note that the pH stays mostly the same until enough base has been added to neutralize the acid. In this plot, the acid is neutralized after about 10 teaspoons of base has been added. This endpoint will vary depending on the concentration of acid in the initial solution. If only a little acid is present, the endpoint will occur much sooner; if a lot more acid is present, the endpoint will occur later.

The students will perform a titration in the experiment for this chapter and it will look somewhat like this one. The vertical scale will not be pH, but color change.

How does this help determine the concentration of an unknown base or acid?

Recall that the endpoint is where the base has completely neutralized the acid. If the concentration of the base is known, and from the plot, the volume of base added is also known, then the concentration of acid can be calculated using this simple formula:

(volume of base) x (concentration of base) =
   (volume of acid) x (concentration of acid)

It is not important for the students to grasp this formula at this point. However, they should see the "formula" and know it can be calculated.

## 5.6 Summary

Discuss with the students the following main points of this chapter:

- In an acid-base reaction, the acid and base are neutralized. This means that neither the acid nor the base remains acidic or basic. The neutralization of acids and bases gives salt and water.

- Complete neutralization occurs only when the amount of acid equals the amount of base. When the amount of acid equals the amount of base, the resulting solution is neutral.

- The concentration of an unknown acid or base can be determined by doing a titration. This simply means that because equal amounts of acid and base neutralize each other, an unknown concentration of base (or acid) can be determined using a known concentration of acid (or base). Experiment 5 illustrates this concept.

Experiment 5 : Vinegar and ammonia in the balance:  Date:
An introduction to titrations

Objective:  *To determine how much ammonia is needed to change the color of vinegar from red to green with the use of an indicator.*

Hypothesis:  *An indicator can be used to observe the acid-base reaction of vinegar and ammonia.*

Materials:
- red cabbage indicator (from Experiment 4)
- household ammonia
- vinegar
- small jars
- measuring spoons

Experiment:

1. Measure out 1/4 cup of vinegar and put it into one of the small jars.

2. Add enough of the red cabbage indicator to get a deep red color.

3. With the measuring spoons, carefully add one teaspoon of the ammonia to the vinegar solution.  Swirl gently and record the color of the solution.

4. Add another teaspoon of ammonia to the vinegar and record the color of the solution.

5. Keep adding ammonia to the vinegar and record the color of the solution for every teaspoon you add.

6. When the color has changed from red to green, stop adding ammonia.

7. Plot the data on the graph.  The horizontal axis should be labeled "Teaspoons of Ammonia" and the vertical axis should be labeled "Color of Solution."

In this experiment, the students will perform an acid-base titration using a cabbage water indicator.

In this experiment the students will write their own hypothesis.  Help them think about the material in this section and write a suitable hypothesis. An example is given.

The red cabbage indicator from Experiment 4 is required.  If the indicator is too old (more than several weeks, or has mold or bacteria growing in it), fresh cabbage indicator should be made. (See Chapter 4.)

A large glass jar is recommended for the titration.

An eye dropper can be used instead of measuring spoons if desired but students will need to add droperfuls instead of "drops."

NOTE:

This titration can be tricky if the concentration of the base is too dilute.  A quick test can be performed by the teacher without the students' observation.  Take the 1/4 cup of vinegar and add indicator to the mixture.  See that it turns red.  Add the 1/4 cup ammonia directly to the acid-indicator mixture.  The color should turn green, but if the color is still red, add another 1/4 cup of ammonia.  It should turn green; however, if it does not, dilute the vinegar with 1/2 cup water and repeat the above steps.  This quick "titration" will help determine how much total ammonia is needed to neutralize the acid.  A 1/4 cup is equal to roughly 12-14 teaspoons.  Adjust the titration so that not much more than 1/4 cup is needed.  Less is all right, but the students will get frustrated if they have to add more than 20 teaspoons; and the best part of the titration is the last part.

8. For every teaspoon added, mark the graph with a round dot the corresponding color.

9. When all of the data have been plotted, connect the dots.

Results:

| Number of Teaspoons | Color |
| --- | --- |
| 1 | red |
| 2 | red |
| 3 | red |
| 4 | red |
| 5 | red |
| 6 | red |
| 7 | red |
| 8 | red |
| 9 | red/purple |
| 10 | red/purple |
| 11 | purple/green |
| 12 | green |
| 13 | green |
| 14 | green |
| 15 | green |
| 16 | green |

Have the students record the color of the solution with each teaspoonful of ammonia added. The color stays mostly red, then a little purple, and finally turns all green. The transition is quite striking.

Have the students continue adding ammonia to prove see that the color stays green.

_____
_____
_____
_____
_____
_____
_____
_____
_____
_____
_____
_____
_____
_____
_____
_____
_____
_____
_____
_____
_____
_____
_____
_____

*Extra page for more data to be collected if necessary.*

Graphing your data:

On the graph below record the number of teaspoons (horizontal axis) corresponding to the color of the solution (vertical axis).

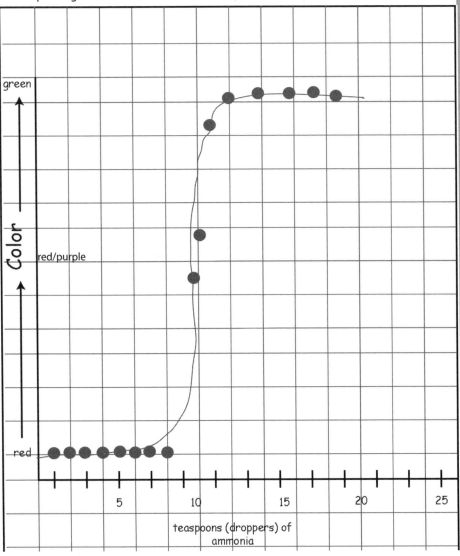

The data should look something like that shown in the plot. Many points lie along the bottom left of the plot, then one or two points will be in the middle. Finally, several will be along the top right-hand edge of the plot.

Have the students connect the points with a smooth curved line. Their plot should look similar to the plot in this section. Point out the following points on the graph:

1. Left-hand lower portion of the plot, the solution is acidic.

2. Middle portion, where the line is going upward, the solution is between acidic and basic (near neutral).

3. Upper right-hand corner, the solution is basic.

Point out that we know this because the color of the indicator is known at various pH values, as we observed in Chapter 4.

Conclusions:

*It took 15 teaspoons to turn the solution green.*
*It took 15 teaspoons to neutralize the vinegar with ammonia.*
*The amount of ammonia required to neutralize the vinegar was equal*
*to the amount of vinegar used.*

Help the students make valid conclusions.  Some examples are given.
Have the students write down the amount of ammonia it took to
neutralize the vinegar.  Note whether this equals the amount of vinegar
that was used (1/4 cup).   Here are some equivalent amounts:

> 3 tsp. = 1 T
> 4 T = 1/4 cup
> 12 tsp. = 1/4 cup
> 1 tsp. = 2 droppers full

Depending on the brands of vinegar and ammonia used, the amounts are
often equal.

## Review

Define the following terms:

neutralization reaction    *One type of exchange reaction such as an acid-base reaction.*

concentration    *The number of molecules in a given volume.*

concentrated    *Many molecules in a given volume.*

dilute    *Few molecules in a given volume.*

Glacial acetic acid    *Concentrated acetic acid.*

indigestion    *Stomach pain caused by excess acid.*

titration    *An experimental technique; can be used to determine concentration for acid-base reaction.*

axes (axis)    *The vertical and horizontal lines on a plot that tell what is to be plotted.*

*NOTES:*

# Chapter 6: Mixtures

Time Required:

      Text reading - 1 hour
      Experimental - 30 minutes

Experimental setup:

      NONE

Additional Materials:

      Vinegar
      Vegetable oil
      Rubbing alcohol
      Ammonia
      Melted butter

*Overall Objectives:*

In this chapter the students will learn about different types of mixtures and what makes something mix or not mix.

## 6.1 Introduction

Most of the things we encounter in daily life are mixtures, rather than pure substances. The example given is cake. From the outside, cake looks like it is one substance, but it is actually a mixture of many different things.

Discuss with the students other things that are mixtures such as other foods, shampoo, most commercial cleaning fluids, and concrete.

JUST FOR FUN

Have the students bake a cake and let them mix the ingredients:

All natural substances like eggs, flour, milk and chocolate are also mixtures of many different kinds of molecules.

### Easy Chocolate Cake

2 cups sugar
3/4 cup shortening
2 eggs
3 cups flour
2 teaspoons baking soda

1 tsp. salt
1/2 cup cocoa
1 cup buttermilk
1 cup boiling water

Add dry ingredients with 1 cup buttermilk. Beat until smooth. Mix in 1 cup boiling water mixed with two teaspoons of baking soda. Bake at 350 degrees for 25 to 30minutes. Makes three layers.

## 6.2 Types of mixtures

Two types of mixtures are discussed. They are homogeneous mixtures and heterogeneous mixtures. Homogeneous mixtures are mixtures where the molecules are evenly distributed throughout the mixture. Saltwater is an example of a homogeneous mixture. Other examples include the following:

> alchohol-water mixtures
> sugar-water mixtures
> vinegar
> household ammonia

Heterogeneous mixtures are those mixtures where the molecules are not evenly distributed throughout the mixture. Ice water is an example of a heterogeneous mixture. Other examples include:

> sand
> concrete
> ice cream floats
> salad dressing

Another mixture that looks homogeneous but is actually heterogeneous is milk. Milk is a colloid. A colloid has very small molecules suspended in it that are not evenly distributed in solution and are too small to see with our eyes. All colloids are heterogeneous and are cloudy. True homogeneous solutions are clear or colored but not cloudy.

## 6.3 Like dissolves like

"Like" in this context means that both substances are either polar or charged. (See next page for definition of "polar.")

"Unlike" means that one substance is made of polar, or charged, molecules and the other is made of nonpolar, or uncharged, molecules.

The rule states that substances that are alike will dissolve in one another and substances that are not alike will not dissolve in one another.

A molecule with a positive (+) end and a (-) end is a polar molecule.

Polar simply means having two opposite directions or natures. In the case of molecules, polar means that there are two oppositely charged ends.

Water is very polar. All OH ends are also very polar wherever they occur on a molecule. Molecules with these OH ends will easily mix with water. Methanol (wood alcohol) has the structure $CH_3$-OH and mixes easily with water because of the OH at the end.

Other molecules that are also polar in water are acetic acid and sugar. Both of these molecules contain polar OH groups, and both easily dissolve in water.

Most of the vegetable oil molecule is not charged. Point out the long chains (blue) and discuss that these chains are not polar (charged). The C-O bonds (red) in the vegetable oil are slightly polar, but not polar enough to allow the oil to dissolve in water.

Mineral oil is made of only carbons and hydrogens. This molecule has no polar groups at all and will not dissolve in water.

Many cleaning fluids are based on the principle that like dissolves like. Cleaning fluids that are used to clean things other than water-based products are generally nonpolar. Mineral oil cleans oil-based paints because mineral oil is nonpolar.

## 6.4 Soap

The most common soap or detergent is SDS (sodium dodecyl sulfate or sodium lauryl sufate). Many soaps, shampoos, and detergents contain SDS, and it will be listed as a primary ingredient.

The main point to emphaisize in this section is that soap "allows" oils to dissolve in water. It does this by forming tiny oil droplets that are suspended in the surrounding water. These little oil droplets can then be washed away by the excess water.

## 6.5 Summary

Discuss with the students the following main points for this chapter:

- There are main two types of mixtures: homogeneous and heterogeneous. Homogeneous mixtures are the same throughout and heterogeneous mixtures are not.

- If two things are "like" each other, they will mix more readily than with things that are not alike.

- Things that are alike will dissolve in each other. Dissolve means to loosen and separate the molecules of one substance so that it can mix into another substance.

- Soap can mix with both oil and water. This allows soap to "dissolve" oil in water.

Experiment 6:          Mix it up!                Date: _____

Objective:    *We will observe which solutions mix and which do not.*
_____

Hypothesis:    *Oil will not dissolve in water without soap.*
*Vegetable oil and butter will mix, but oil and water will not mix.*
_____

Materials:
    vinegar
    rubbing alcohol
    ammonia
    vegetable oil
    melted butter
    several small jars
    food coloring
    dish soap

Experiment:

Part I:  See what mixes.

1. The grid in the Results section is labeled with the following terms along the top and sides of the grid.: water, vinegar, rubbing alcohol, ammonia, vegetable oil, and melted butter,

2. Take out 6 small jars and add 1/4 cup of each item to separate jars. Label the jars.

3. Add a drop of food coloring to each jar.

4. Mix one tablespoon of the uncolored items with 1 tablespoon of each colored item. Record in the boxes whether or not the two items mix.

In this experiment the students will observe different mixtures.

The objective is left blank. To help the students write a suitable objective for this experiment, have them first read the experiment carefully. A suggested objective is listed.

The hypothesis is also left blank. Help the students write a suitable hypothesis. To help them, discuss the main points of this chapter:

- most things are mixtures
- like dissolves like
- soap helps oil dissolve in water

Two suggestions are given.

Materials:

Any of these items can be substituted for other solutions if needed. Try to pick at least two "oily" items and two water-based items.

Results:

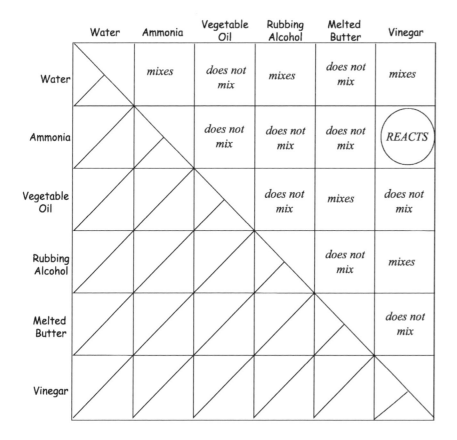

| | Water | Ammonia | Vegetable Oil | Rubbing Alcohol | Melted Butter | Vinegar |
|---|---|---|---|---|---|---|
| Water | | mixes | does not mix | mixes | does not mix | mixes |
| Ammonia | | | does not mix | does not mix | does not mix | REACTS |
| Vegetable Oil | | | | does not mix | mixes | does not mix |
| Rubbing Alcohol | | | | | does not mix | mixes |
| Melted Butter | | | | | | does not mix |
| Vinegar | | | | | | |

Have the students fill in the grid and note which solutions mix and which do not.

The groups that will mix are as follows:

- water, ammonia, rubbing alcohol, and vinegar

- vegetable oil and melted butter

NOTE:
Ammonia and vingear will react. This is an acid base reaction. They also mix.

Part II:  Soap, oil, and water.
1. Put 1/4 cup of water into one of the small glass jars.  Add one drop of food coloring.
2. Add 1 tablespoon of vegetable oil to the water.
3. Mix the water and oil.  Record your results.
4. Add 1 tablespoon of liquid dish soap to the oil/water mixture.
5. Mix thoroughly.  Record your results.
6. Add another tablespoon of liquid dish soap to the mixture, and mix thoroughly.
7. Record your results.

Results:

Oil + water:      *The oil and water do not mix.*


Oil + water + 1T soap:  *The solution is cloudy.  Some oil has disappeared, but most of the oil is still visible.*


Oil + water + 2T soap:  *The solution is even more cloudy, and more oil has disappeared.*

In this section the students will experiment with soap to dissolve an oil-water mixture.

As mentioned earlier, soap will make a colloidal mixture of oil and water. This will be visible as the soap turns the oil-water mixture cloudy.  There will also be some bubbles, but overall, the mixture should begin to turn cloudy.

As more soap is added, less free oil is visible.

Conclusions:

_Oil does not mix with water._

_Oil forms a heterogeneous mixture with water._

_Alcohol mixes with water. Alcohol is "like" water._

_Vegetable oil dissolves in butter. Vegetable oil and butter are "like" each other._

_Vegetable oil and butter are both "not like" water._

Help the students make valid conclusions based on the data they have collected.

Some suggestions are given.

Help the students make conclusions using the ideas presented in this chapter. Have the students decide which solutions are "like" each other and which are not. Have them record these as their observations.

Review

Define the following terms:

mixture    *Two or more pure  substances mixed together.*

homogeneous    *A mixture of the "same kind," like saltwater.*

heterogeneous    *A mixture of  the "other kind," like ice water.*

dissolve    *When two or more substances like to mix.*

What does the phrase "like dissolves like" mean? *Two solutions that are "like"*
*each other will dissolve in each other.  Two that are not alike, will not dissolve.*

Name two molecules with charged ends.    *water and salt*

Name two molecules without charged ends.    *vegetable oil and mineral oil*

How does soap work? *Soap is a molecule with a charged end and an*
*uncharged end.  Uncharged molecules will dissolve in the uncharged end of a soap*
*molecule, and charged molecules will dissolve in the charged end.  A micelle will*
*form, with the oil on the inside, surrounded by water.  The oil can then be washed*
*away.*

Draw a micelle.

*NOTES:*

# Chapter 7: Separating Mixtures

Time Required:

    Text reading - 1 hour
    Experimental - 30 minutes

Experimental setup:

    NONE

Additional Materials:

    Ballpoint pens
    Rubbing alcohol
    Cardboard shoebox

## Overall Objectives:

Separating mixtures is very important in chemistry; it is a large part of the discipline of Analytical Chemistry. This chapter will introduce several simple techniques used to separate mixtures. These include filtration, evaporation, and chromatography.

## 7.1 Introduction

Discuss with the students how they might separate different mixtures.

For example,

How would you separate Legos and rocks? *by hand*

How would you separate sand and rocks? *with a sieve*

How would you separate sand and water? *let the water dry out*

Explain to the students that there are different ways to separate mixtures and that they will learn about three: filtration, evaporation, and chromatography.

## 7.2 Filtration

Filtration is one way to separate mixtures of different sizes. Some common household filters include sieves, cheesecloth, and coffee filters.

The pore size of the filter determines the sizes of things that can be separated. Large pore sizes like those found in sieves, can separate liquids from larger solids like spaghetti or broccoli. It is even possible

with a sieve to separate flour from rice. In this case the sieve would also need to be shaken to loosen the flour from around the rice.

Some examples of molecular sieves include the pores in cell membranes. Cells have tiny holes that allow small molecules, like salt, to flow freely in and out. Larger molecules (like proteins and DNA) cannot get through these pores and are kept inside the cell.

## 7.3 Evaporation

Evaporation can be used to separate two substances if only one of them evaporates. Salts and water can be separated this way since water evaporates and salt does not. Alcohol and water cannot be separated using this technique since both alcohol and water evaporate. Baking soda and salt cannot be separated this way since neither baking soda nor salt can evaporate.

To explain evaporation, the next section introduces the three basic states of matter: solids, liquids and gases.

## 7.4 Solids, liquids, and gases

Matter exists in three states: solid, liquid, and gas. For water, these states differ in how tightly packed the molecules are and in how much energy the molecules have. For solid water, ice, the molecules are packed into a crystalline lattice. The molecules in ice are actually less densely packed than in liquid water. However, the water molecules in ice have less energy (and hence are colder) than those in liquid water.

As energy is added to the ice, the water molecules begin to shake and wiggle. This partially overcomes the weak forces that hold the molecules together in a crystal. The water molecules become able to slide past each other and move around. They lose their crystalline order but still remain densely packed. This is what a liquid looks like on the molecular scale.

As more energy is added, the water molecules completely overcome the forces holding them together, and the free molecules move away from each other as a gas. This is what happens during evaporation. The water molecules spread out so thin they are no longer perceptibly different from the air.

## 7.5 Chromatography

Chromatography is another way to separate mixtures.

Molecules will often "stick" to a solid; we say they adsorb to the solid. Molecules that adsorb differently (either strongly or weakly) to a solid (matrix) of some kind can be separated by chromatography. The matrix can be any porous material from paper to specially designed columns used to adsorb gas molecules. The mixture to be separated (ink colors, large molecules, gases, etc.) is exposed to one end of the matrix and allowed to migrate towards the other end. As the solution (or gas) passes over the paper (or column), molecules will move at different speeds, depending on how strongly they adsorb. The faster moving molecules move ahead of the slower moving molecules, separating them.

## 7.6 Summary

Discuss with the students the following main points of this chapter:

- There are many ways to separate mixutures. This chapter . discusses three: filtration, evaporation, and chromatography.

- Filtration uses filters to separate things of different size. A filter can be anything from a metal sieve to a paper coffee filter. The holes in a filter are called pores. The pore size determines what can be separated. Small pores, like those found in coffee filters, can separate water from coffee. However, a sieve cannot be used to separate coffee from water because the pores are too big.

- Evaporation can be used to separate things that evaporate from things that don't. Water evaporates and salt does not, so evaporation can be used to separate salt from water.

- Paper chromatography can be used to separate the colors in ink. This is demostrated in Experiment 7.

- Discuss with the students the three states of matter: solids, liquids, and gases. Discuss how water can be a solid (ice), a liquid (water), and a gas (water vapor or steam). Other things also exist in different states. Carbon dioxide, for example, is a gas at room temperature. However, dry ice is carbon dioxide in solid form.

Experiment 7:      Black is black?        Date: _____

Objective:    *To determine the individual colors in various ink mixtures.*
_____

Hypothesis:    *Black ink contains only black ink and no other colors.*
              *Black ink contains all of the colors.*

Materials:
        ball point ink pens of various colors, including black
        rubbing alcohol
        coffee filters (white)
        small jars

Experiment:

1. Pour 1/4 cup of alcohol into several small jars.

2. Take the ink pens and remove the thin plastic tube from the inside.

3. Pull off the top or cut the plastic tube in half.

4. Take the tube and swirl the end of it in the alcohol. Watch that some of the color gets dissolved in the alcohol, but don't let it get too colored.

5. Cut the coffee filter paper into thin strips 1/4 to 1/2 inch wide and 5 to 6 inches long.

6. Place the ends of the strips into the dissolved ink in the jars and allow the alcohol to migrate upwards. It is fine for the strips to touch the sides of the glass jar, but the alcohol won't migrate past this point. It is better if you can suspend the strips in the alcohol without letting the sides touch. To do this tape the strips to the inside of a cardboard box and suspend them in the glass jars.

7. The colors in the ink will migrate up the absorbent strips. Let the strips sit in the alcohol overnight.

In this experiment the students will use paper chromatography to separate the individual colors in inks.

Have the students state an objective. To do this, they need to read through the experiment before beginning. An example is given.

Have the students state a hypothesis. Specifically ask them to predict what colors will be in black ink. Ask them what colors they think black ink contains. Help them write a hypothesis based on their prediction. Some examples are given.

Multicolored ballpoint pens work best. Try to find one with at least 7 or 8 different colors. Don't buy an expensive pen because it will be taken apart for the experiment. If a multicolored pen cannot be found, regular Bic® pens can be used. Black, blue, red and green will give enough colors to compare. Ballpoint pens work better than felt tip pens or markers.

It is important not to let the color of the alcohol-ink mixture get too dark. A quick swirl with the open end of the pen is usually enough.

The ink will not migrate past the point where the paper touches the side of the jar. To avoid holing up the ink's progress place the jars on the inside of a cardboard box with the papers suspended from above the solutions.

Results:

Tape the strips of paper below.
Write the original ink color and record the different colors that each is made of.

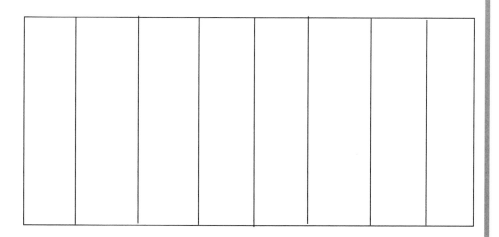

After the ink has had a chance to migrate up the paper and once the paper has dried, the students can tape them directly into the book.

Have the students write the original ink color directly on the paper and then write which colors have separated out of the ink.

Have them note which colors make up black. Depending on the brand of pen, the black ink should show all colors or nearly all colors. Brown also shows all colors.

Most of the other colors will be a mixture of fewer colors. Depending on the brand of pen, these colors may also be a mixture of similar colors. For example, a blue pen may show a mixture of only a dark blue and a light blue.

Repeat the previous steps with an unknown sample of ink. Compare your results with those above and try to determine the colors in your unknown ink sample.

| Unknown |
| Color in the unknown: |

Now give the students an unknown. Make the unknown without letting the students observe. The unknown can contain inks from two different pens. If a mixture of two colors is to be used, first swirl each in alcohol and then mix the two alcohol solutions.

Suggest that the students give you an unknown. Several unknowns can be set up overnight.

Using the pattern of colors from the known pens, help the students try to identify which pen was used for the unknown.

Conclusions:

_____

_____

_____

_____

_____

_____

_____

_____

_____

Help the students make valid conclusions based on the data they have collected. Help them be specific. For example,

- Black ink from Brand X is made of red, yellow, black, and brown.

- Red ink from Brand X is made of red and pink.

- Blue ink from Brand Y has only blue ink in it.

Ask whether or not they proved or disproved their hypothesis.

Discuss those conclusions that are not valid. For example,

- All black ink has yellow in it. This is not valid based on these data; not all black ink has been tested.

- Blue inks contain only blue. Again, not all blue inks have been tested.

Have the students write any sources of error. For example,

- All of my alcohol went away and no dye went up the paper.

- The papers fell off the box and into the solution.

Review

Define the following terms:

sieve    *A metal bowl with holes in it; a type of filter.*

filter    *Anything that can be used to separate things of different sizes, such as coffee filters, mesh, sieves, or cheesecloth.*

filtration    *A process to separate things of different size.*

pore    *The holes in a filter.*

solid state    *The state of matter ihat exists when the molecules are tightly packed.*

gaseous state    *The state of matter in which the molecules are apart from each other.*

liquid state    *The state between the gaseous state and the solid state; the molecules are more loosely packed than in a solid.*

chromatography    *A technique used to separate different moleclues.*

separation    *The process of taking one or more things out of a mixture.*

*NOTES:*

## Chapter 8:  Energy Molecules

Time Required:

      Text reading - 1 hour
      Experimental - 30 minutes

Experimental setup:

      NONE

Additional Materials:

      Raw foods such as:
         bread
         celery
         banana
         potato

## Overall Objectives:

This chapter will introduce "energy" molecules. Energy molecules are those molecules that fuel our bodies, such as carbohydrates and starches.

## 8.1 Introduction

Some of the words are difficult to pronounce and can be intimidating. Also, these molecules are more complicated than those we have examined previously. It is not important that the students remember all of the names or understand all of the chemical structures. The main points are as follows:

- Carbohydrates are energy molecules.

- Carbohydrates are made mostly of carbon, hydrogen, and oxygen.

- Small carbohydrates are sugars.

- Large carbohydrates are starches and cellulose.

- Starches and cellulose are long chains of smaller carbohydrates (sugars).

## 8.2 Nutrients

Discuss the various types of foods we eat to get our *nutrients* (i.e., those foods that help our bodies grow and live). Have the students list some of their favorite foods and ask them what kinds of nutrients they think those foods might have. For example,

Carrots have vitamin A.
Milk and meat have protein.
Oranges and lemons have vitamin C.
Eggs have protein.
Milk and sardines have calcium.

## 8.3 Carbohydrates

Carbohydrates are made of carbon atoms and water molecules. For example, glucose, a simple sugar, has 6 carbons, 6 oxygens, and 12 hydrogens. A chemical formula for glucose can be written as $C_6(H_2O)_6$. This formula shows that glucose has 6 carbon atoms and 6 molecules of water. This is the origin of the name "carbo-hydrate."

The simple carbohydrates are the monocacharides (mon-o-sac´cha-rides).
Larger carbohydrates are the oligosaccharides (o-li-go-sac´cha-rides).

Monosaccharides are very important for our metabolism. They are an essential component in many biochemical pathways. For humans, simple sugars are essential for brain development. Human milk, for example, has the highest sugar content of all animal milk. Whale and seal milk have lower sugar content and higher fat content than human milk, since fat is essential for protecting these animals from the cold ocean waters.

## 8.4 Starches

The largest carbohydrates are the polysaccharides (pol-y-sac´cha-rides) which include the starches and cellulose.

The two main energy molecules found in plants, that can be used by humans, are amylose (am´-y-lose) and amylopectin (am´y-lo-pec-tin). These are the two main starches found in potatoes, breads, and pasta.

Amylose has several thousand  glucose units hooked together into a long chain or polymer.  For simplicity these are shown as straight chains in the picture, but the real amylose chains are twisted around to form an irregular helical coil.

Amylopectin also contains several thousand glucose units, but instead of being a helical coil, it is branched.  The structure for glycogen is very similar to that of amylopectin.

In the experiment that the students will perform for this chapter, it is amylose that is detected by iodine.  Amylopectin, glycogen, and cellulose cannot be detected by iodine.  The helical coil of amylose interacts with the iodine molecules to give a deep purple or black color.  The other starches do not form this coil and therefore cannot be detected by iodine.

## 8.5 Cellulose

Cellulose is the main structural molecule for plants.  Because plants need to have rigid cell walls for support (since they don't have bones),  the structure for cellulose is very different from that of starches.

The main difference between the bonding for the starches and cellulose is the orientation of the linkage between individual glucose units.  For the starches, the term "down" is given for the students.  The actual name of this type of bond is "alpha," and it ahs the symbol $\alpha$.  Starches have $\alpha$ bonds between their glucose units.

The term given to the students for the bonds between the glucose units for cellulose is "up." The actual name for this type of bond is "beta," and it has the symbol $\beta$.  Starches have $\beta$ bonds between their glucose units.

This small difference in how the units are hooked to each other makes a huge difference in their overall shape.  As mentioned earelier, the starches are either coils or large branched molecules. In contrast, cellulose molcules form large sheets which can stack on one another. The cell walls in plants are made of layers of parallel cellulose sheets. These layers make the cell wall rigid.

Humans cannot use cellulose for energy molecules.  We do not have the necessary enzymes required to break the $\beta$ linkages of cellulose glucose units.  Certain animals have bacteria that break the cellulose linkages for them, so they can simply eat grasses and other plants for their diet. Humans get other nutrients from plants but need to eat other foods for energy molecules.

## 8.6 Summary

Discuss with the students the following main points of this chapter:

- Carbohydrates are molecules found in potatoes, pasta, and breads that give our bodies "energy." These molecules are made of sugar molecules. The sugar molecules are used by our bodies for energy.

- The smaller carbohydrates, called simple carbohydrates, are the sugars, like fructose and glucose. These are single sugars and provide "quick" energy for our bodies since they are easily broken down. The larger carbohydrates, like starch and amylose, are made of many sugar molecules linked together in a long chain. The fact that they are in a long chain means that they are less quickly used by our bodies, and they can serve as stored energy for later use.

- Cellulose is another large carbohydrate molecule found in grass and other plants. It provides plants cells with rigid walls for stability. Humans cannot use grass as a source of energy because we cannot break the linkages between the glucose units in a cellulose molecule. Cows, horses, and other animals can use grass for food energy because they have bacteria in their gut which breaks the bonds for them.

*NOTES:*

Experiment 8:     Show me the starch          Date:

Objective:     *To determine which foods contain starch.*

Hypothesis:     *Potatoes conatin starch.  Celery does not.*

Materials:
> tincture of iodine
> variety of foods including:
>> pasta
>> bread
>> celery
>> banana
>> potato
>> other fruits
> laundry starch
> absorbent paper
> eye dropper
> [Iodine is VERY poisonous, do not eat any food items with iodine.]

Experiment:

1. Take several food items and place them on a cookie sheet.

2. Take the liquid starch and, with the eye dropper, put a small amount on a piece of absorbent paper and label it "Control." Let it dry.

3. Add a droplet of iodine to the starch on the control paper. Record the color.

4. Add iodine to each of the food items and record the color.

5. Compare the color on the "control" to the color of each food item.

6. Note those food items that change color and those that do not.

In this experiment the students will determine which foods contain starch (amylose) and which do not.

Have the student write the objective and hypothesis. Have them guess which foods might have starch and which might not, based on the text for this chapter. Some examples are given.

Only amylose is detected by iodine, so technically students will be observing only those foods that contain amylose. Iodine is very poisonous so warn the students not to eat any foods that have iodine on them.

Select a variety of food items. Include some that contain amylose, like potatoes or bread. Laundry starch is used as a control. Laundry starch is made of corn starch (which contains amylose) and borax, so it can be used as a positive control. Some papers have amylose in them, so you also need to test the paper alone. Use a paper that does not turn black.

Explain the use of a control to the students. Controls test the experimental method to see if it's working. If the control does not work, something is wrong with the experiment and any other results are not valid. If the control works, then it is more likely that the results of the experiment are real and can be used to draw final conclusions. For example, if the iodine solution were bad, old, or just not working, then even the laundry starch would not turn black. But if no control was performed, the results might indicate that nothing has starch in it. These results would be incorrect, and the conclusion that "potatoes have no starch" would be incorrect. Control experiments are a very important part of real scientific investigation. They are essential for determining the validity of individual experiments.

**Results:**

| Control | Food Item | Color |
|---------|-----------|-------|
| | | |
| | | |
| | | |
| | | |
| | | |
| | | |
| | | |
| | | |
| | | |
| | | |
| | | |
| | | |
| | | |
| | | |
| | | |
| | | |
| | | |
| | | |
| | | |

Have the students record their results. Those items containing starch should have a deep purple, almost black color. Everything else will stay light brown.

Conclusions:

_____
_____
_____
_____
_____
_____
_____

Help the students write valid conclusions based on the data they have collected.  Have them write down if they proved  or disproved their hypothesis.

Some example are:

- Raw potatoes turn black with iodine.
- Potatoes contain starch.
- Raw celery does not turn iodine black.
- Celery does not have starch.  [starch here meaning amylose]

OPTIONAL:

Test several items before and after cooking them.  Ask the students to predict whether or not cooking will affect the outcome of their results.

Cooking breaks the bonds between glucose units and they should see a difference with cooked foods.  Cooked foods should not turn purple.

Review

Define the following terms:

nutrients        *Essential molecules we get from the foods we eat.*

carbohydrate     *Molecule made with carbon, oxygen, and hydrogen.*

monosaccharide   *Molecules of a single sugar like glucose.*

oligosaccharide  *Molecules formed by a "few" sugars, like sucrose; table sugar.*

polysaccharide   *"Many" sugars, like starches and cellulose.*

starch    *Long chains of sugar units; found in plants and animals.*

cellulose    *Long chains of sugar units; found mostly in plants.*

amylose    *A common polysaccharide found in plants such as potatoes.*

amylopectin    *A polysaccharide found in plants.*

*NOTES:*

# Chapter 9: Polymers

Time Required:

    Text reading - 1 hour
    Experimental - 30 minutes

Experimental setup:

    NONE

Additional Materials:

    NONE

## Overall Objectives:

This chapter introduces polymers. A polymer is any molecule that consists of several repeating units. In the last chapter, energy molecules (carbohydrates) were polymers of glucose units.

The main points from this chapter are as follows:

- Polymers are long molecules of repeating units.

- A polymer's shape determines its properties.

- Polymers can be modified to change properties.

## 9.1 Introduction

Explain to the students that polymers are long chains of repeating units. Review with them the Greek word root for "poly" and "mer" and explain that *polymer* literally means "many parts."

Discuss with the students items that they know are made of plastic. For example,

    toys
    plastic wrap
    parts of cars
    CD players
    video cases

Explain to them that all of these things are made of polymers.

Have the students discuss those things that might be made of polymers.

These include all plastics, things made of wood, foods, and clothing. Even our bodies contain polymers. (See next chapter.)

Explain to them that there are many different kinds of polymers, both natural and synthetic. Polymers can be chains of identical repeating units like cellulose and starch, but they can also have different kinds of repeating units. (See next chapter.)

## 9.2 Polymer uses

As we saw in the last chapter, the structure of polymers helps determine its physical properties. Recall that cellulose and starch are made of exactly the same molecules but they are put together differently. This gives them very different properties.

Explain to the students that the different properties that polymers can have makes them very useful. Discuss with them some soft and hard polymers they may know. Explain that these differences are due to differences in the polymer structure.

## 9.3 Structure of polymers

Differences in structure also affect the properties of synthetic polymers. For example, plastics made of linear chains of polyethylene ("linear" refers to those without side branches) are very different from chains made that contain side branches. Linear chains can pack closely, which makes the plastic hard and stiff. Branched molecules, on the other hand, cannot pack together tightly, and this makes the plastic soft.

Some other polymers that are commonly used include the following:

- polypropylene — used in the textile industry to make molds

- polyisoprene — synthetic rubbers

- polystyrene — toys

- polyvinyl chloride — foams, films, and fibers.

## 9.4 Modifying polymers

Polymer properties can also change simply by hooking the individual polymer chains together.

Explain to the students that the vulcanization of rubber is one such process.

When natural rubber is heated in the presence of sulfur, the long linear chains connect with each other via sulfur bonds. This changes the physical properties of natural rubber.

The vulcanization of rubber causes cross-links in the polymer molecules. They are called cross-links because they link two molecules across the chains.

The number of cross-links can be varied by changing the amount of sulfur added, the heat, and the time the process is allowed.

Rubber products, like surgical gloves and kitchen gloves, are made when few cross-links are added to natural rubber. When more cross-links are added, the rubber becomes stiff enough for bicycle tubes and tires.

Also, the nature of the cross-links gives rubber its elasticity. Rubber bands can be stretched, which stretches out the long polymer chains. However, because of the cross-links, the rubber bands snap back to their original shape and size when released.

## 9.5 Summary

Discuss with the students the following main points of this chapter:

- "Polymer" is a general term describing many different molecules. Polymers include the carbohydrates from Chapter 8, plastics, and proteins and DNA from Chapter 10.

- Polymers can be put together in different ways. They can be long, linear chains, they can have side branches, or they can be connected to each other. These different shapes give polymers different properties.

- Polymer properties can be modified with chemicals or heat. Review with the students the changes that occur when natural rubber is heated. This process is called vulcanization. [The word vulcanization comes from the name of the Roman god of fire, Vulcan.]

Experiment 9:                  Gooey glue                  Date: _____

Objective:   *In this experiment we will observe a change in properties as*
             *two polymers are added together.*

Hypothesis:  *Liquid starch will change the polymer properties of white*
             *Elmer's glue.  No difference will be observed between the*
             *two glues.*

Materials:
        liquid laundry starch
        Elmer's white glue
        Elmer's blue glue ( or another glue different from white glue)
        small jars (3-4)
        marker
        popsicle stick for stirring

Experiment:

Part I

1.  Open the bottle of Elmer's white glue.  Put a small amount on your fingertips. Note the color and consistency (sticky, dry, hard, soft) of the glue.  Record your observations.

2.  Now look carefully at the liquid starch.  Pour a small amount out on your fingers or in a jar.  Note the color and consistency of the starch.  Record your observations.

3.  Take one of the jars and put 4 tablespoons of water into it.

4.  Note the level of water in the jar and draw a small line with a marker at the water level.

5.  Add another 4 tablespoons of water and mark the water level with a marker.

6.  Empty out the water.

Have the students state an objective and an hypothesis.  Have the students read the experiment before writing these.

In this experiment the students will combine Elmer's white glue with liquid laundry starch.  The liquid laundry starch will change the properties of the glue and create something like "silly putty," a soft maleable ball.  The blue glue does not react in exactly the same manner.  Have the students predict if there will be a difference between blue glue and white glue.

Because Elmer's glue is difficult to measure, steps 3-6 provide a way to measure a given amount of glue directly into the jar. The amount of starch added is not that important, but this is given as a guide.  The time the glue stays in the starch is more critical-- more time in the starch results in a stiffer glue-starch "ball."

7. Fill the jar to the first mark with Elmer's glue.

8. Fill the jar to the second mark with liquid starch.

9. Mix the glue and the starch with the popsicle stick.   Record any changes in consistency and color.

10. Take out the mixture in the jar and knead it with your fingers. Observe the consistency and color and record your results.

## Results:

Observations for Elmer's white glue:

*the glue is sticky, thick, with an odor*

_____

_____

Observations for liquid starch:

*the starch is thin, slippery, and light blue*

_____

_____

Observations for mixture Elmer's white gue and equal amounts of liquid starch:

*the properties of the glue change.  the glue loses its stickyness and*
*forms a clump.*

_____

_____

_____

The consistency of the glue will immediately change upon addition of the laundry starch, but it will still be sticky.  The laundry starch needs to be "kneaded" into the glue.

Once enough laundry starch has been kneaded into the glue, the glue-starch ball can be removed from the jar.

Have the students note the change in the properties of the glue and help them think of ways to accurately describe the texture of the glue-starch ball:

- bouncy
- stretchy
- somewhat elastic like a rubber band
- blue/white in color

The mixture continues to get harder as the glue is allowed to react with the starch.  Make more than one glue-starch ball and allow one to be mixed for a longer time, for comparison.

Part II

1. Now take another jar and fill it to the first mark with the Elmer's blue glue.

2. Now add liquid starch to the second level.

3. Mix.

4. Record your observations.


Results:

Observations for mixture of blue glue and liquid starch: _____

___ *the blue glue becomes hardened and not rubbery like the white glue.* ___

_____

_____

_____

Repeat the experiment using a different kind of glue. Elmer's blue glue works best, but any other brand of nonwhite glue can be used.

The consistency of the glue-starch mixture is different with clear or "blue" glues than with the white glue.

Conclusions:

_Elmer's white glue changed from sticky to bouncy (stretch, like rubber) when liquid laundry starch was added._

_Elmer's blue glue did not change in the same way as the white glue. The polymers that make up white glue are likely different from the polymers that make up blue glue._

_Elmer's blue glue might be made of different molecules than Elmer's white glue._

Help the students write valid conclusions based on the data they have collected. Some examples are given.

Try to have the students relate the changes of the glue to the information given in the text.

Some conclusions can be inferred statements that are based on the data collected. For example, because the two glues behaved differently, it is possible that the chemical composition of each are different. Also, they have a different color and texture. However, this experiment did NOT prove that they are different chemically even though the experimental data suggest that this might be true. Discuss how additional investigation is needed to conclude anything about the chemical composition of the two types of glue.

Review

Define the following terms:

meros    *Greek word meaning "unit."*

polymer    *A word that means "many units."*

monomer    *A word that means "single unit."*

polyethylene    *"Many" ethylenes. A polymer used to make plastic.*

vulcanization    *A process to harden natural rubber that uses sulfur and heat.*

*NOTES:*

# Chapter 10:  Biological Polymers:
## Protein and DNA

Time Required:

Text reading - 1 hour
Experimental - 30 minutes

Experimental setup:

NONE

Additional Materials:

Bread

## Overall Objectives:

This chapter introduces two biological polymers: proteins and DNA. These are much more complicated molecules than those previously encountered. However, proteins and DNA are extremely important, so this chapter will serve as an introduction.

## 10.1 Introduction

The main points to emphasize are as follows:

- Proteins are polymers of amino acids.

- Protein polymers fold into different shapes.

- Protein shapes are important for their function.

- Many proteins are tiny molecular machines.

- DNA is a polymer of nucleic acids.

- DNA carries the genetic code and serves as the information library for each cell.

## 10.2 Proteins

Amino acids are the repeating units for proteins. All amino acids have the same basic structure, but have different "R" groups. Some amino acids are acidic, others are basic, and yet others have different properties. The "R" groups give amino acids these different properties.

## 10.3 Proteins are amino acid polymers

Protein polymers are connected through peptide bonds. This simply means that the carbonyl group hooks to the amine group. Amino acids are NOT hooked to each other via the "R" groups.

Short chains are called polypeptides and long chains are called proteins.

The shapes of proteins are important. Proteins fold into various shapes which are determined partly by the function that the protein performs.

The example given is kinesin (ki-nee-sin). Kinesin functions as a molecular delivery truck. It takes molecules from one place to another inside cells.

Kinesin has two "feet" (these are actually called heads), with which it moves along a microtubule "road." Microtubules are long strings of smaller proteins that make a large network of "roads" inside cells. Proteins get carried from place to place along these roads. Kinesin literally "walks" along this road one foot (head) at a time, carrying its cargo.

## 10.4 Protein polymers form special shapes

No matter how complicated the protein shape may look from the outside, it is just one folded-up chain on the inside. In the next figure, the picture on the left shows how human salivary amylase looks when all the atoms are shown. It is very compact, with little or no space between the atoms. The picture on the right is a simplified view that shows only the path of the protein chain, without all the extra atoms. It's still complicated, but by looking carefully one can see that there is only one continuous chain. (Notice also the coils. These are a common feature of almost all proteins.)

Even though the folded protein may look like a shapeless blob, it is actually folded very carefully to get the shape needed to carry out its job (or function).

This picture shows a representative drawing of a kinesin molecule carrying a protein cargo. The "road" shown on the right is a helical array of tubulin molecules.

Kinesin is called a molecular motor because it moves things. There are many different kinds of motors inside living cells. Protein motors do

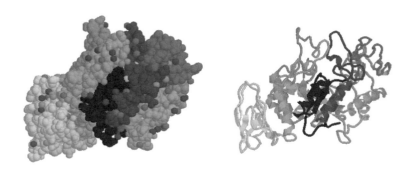

almost all of the work inside the cell. There are motors that cut, motors that build, and motors (like kinesin) that move things. For example, myosin is a motor that looks much like kinesin but is used to power our muscles. Dynein is another motor that powers tiny cilia that keep our lungs clear of dust.

## 10.5  Protein machines

Scientists still do not know all of the proteins inside cells and the roles they play. Many protein assemblies are very complex. Protein machines are very sophisticated motors, rotors, gears, pumps, and scissors. We have not yet learned to build structures with the precision and complexity of these remarkable molecular machines.

Recall that amylose is a starch found in bread and potatoes. In our mouths we have a protein machine called amylase that cuts amylose.

The names of amylose and amylase are very similar. Many enzymes (protein machines) are named after the molecules they work on. Amylase is the enzyme that breaks down amylose, the starch. Notice that the endings differ;" -ase" for the enzyme, "-ose" for the starch.

Enzymes are highly specific. That is, they work only on certain molecules. Amylase does not digest cellulose, only amylose. Cellulase, a different enzyme, digests cellulose. The name of an enzyme usually tells which molecule the enzyme works on.

The blue and green molecule (colored in student text) is the actual structure for human salivary amylase.

## 10.6 DNA

DNA is another biological polymer that is vitally important for all living things. The monomer units that make up DNA are more complicated than the amino acids that form proteins. However, DNA has only a few regular shapes.

## 10.7  DNA structure

DNA is made with nucleotides. These are composed of a ribose sugar and a base. The bases differ, but the sugars are the same for every unit.

There are 4 bases that make up most DNA. They are the following:

- Adenine  A

- Guanine  G

- Cytosine  C

- Thymine  T

When the two strands of the DNA molecule come together (see Section 10.8), the bases line up by forming pairs. Usually A pairs with T and G pairs with C in the ladder.   Two strands of nucleic acid polymer make double-stranded DNA. DNA with only one strand does exist in nature, but it is chemically more susceptible to damage. Thus almost all DNA inside a cell is double stranded. The double-stranded form of DNA stores the genetic code.

In double-stranded DNA, the two strands of nucleic acids pair with the bases in the middle and the sugars on the outside. They then wrap around each other, much like a twisted ladder. These two wrapped polymers form  a structure called a double helix since there are two helices wrapped around each other.

DNA carries the genetic code. The bases, A,C,T, and G code for proteins, which run the cell machinery. The bases can also code for things other than proteins, like signals (start signs and stop signs). DNA is like a big message that tells the cells which proteins to make, how much to make, when to make them, and when to stop. It tells the cells when to grow, when to divide, and when to die. There are many proteins involved in all of these functions, and scientists still do not understand how it all works!

## 10.8 Protein machines on DNA

One of the things that proteins do is copy DNA. This is done by a protein called DNA polymerase.

This is a large protein with lots of amino acids. When it binds to the DNA, it wraps itself around the chain and "holds" the DNA while it makes a copy.

Although DNA polymerases differ slightly between organisms,  their basic shape is the same. They all have a "fingers" and  a "thumb."   The fingers open to admit new nucleotides, and the thumb holds the DNA in place. They also have a "palm" region between the fingers and thumb, which is responsible for the chemical reaction that actually adds new nucleotides.

## 10.9 Summary

Discuss with the students the main points of this chapter. There is a lot of information given in this chapter, and it is not important that the students understand everything presented. However, there are a few main points which the students should remember.

- Proteins and DNA are polymers that are inside every living thing. Proteins are amino-acid polymers, and DNA chains are made of nucleic acids and sugars.

- Proteins do all of the work inside our cells. They have a variety of functions which include moving molecules, synthesizing or making new molecules, and cutting and assembling molecules.

- DNA carries the genetic code. The genetic code is like a large library of information that tells the cells when to grow, when to divide, and what proteins to make.

*NOTES:*

Experiment 10:     Amylase action     Date: _____

Objective: *We will investigate the cutting action of proteins in our saliva.*

Hypothesis: *Saliva will cut the starch molecules in bread.  Iodine will* *not turn bread that has been soaked in saliva black.*

Materials:

    tincture of iodine  [IODINE is poisonous. Do NOT eat.]
    bread
    timer
    wax paper
    marking pen

Experiment:

1. Break the bread into several small pieces.

2. Chew one piece for 30 seconds (use the timer), chew another piece for 1 minute, and a third piece for as long as possible (several minutes).

3. Each time after chewing the bread, spit it onto a piece of wax paper.  Label with the marker the length of time the bread has been chewed.

3. Take a small piece of unchewed bread and place it next to the chewed pieces.

4. Add a drop of iodine to each piece of bread, chewed and unchewed.

5. Record your observations.

6. Take two more pieces of bread.  Collect as much saliva from your mouth as you can (i.e., spit into a cup several times).  Soak both pieces of bread in the saliva.  Place one piece in the refrigerator and leave the other piece at room temperature.  Let them soak for 30 minutes.

7. After 30 minutes add a drop of iodine to each.  Record your results.

In this experiment the students will investigate the digestive process carried out by proteins in saliva.

Have the students read the experiment before writing an objective and hypothesis. Have them look back to Chapter 8 and ask them the following questions:

- What molecule have we studied that is in bread?
  *starch or amylose*

- What happens to food when we put it in our mouth?
  *It begins to be broken down, digested.*

- What do you think happens to amylose in our mouth?
  *It will be broken down, digested.*

- What do you expect iodine to do to unchewed bread?
  *The iodine will turn the starch black.*

- What do you expect the iodine to do to chewed bread?
  *The iodine will not turn it black.*

- Why?
  *Amylose needs to be in a helical shape in order for iodine to turn it black.  If amylose is broken apart, the  helical shape is destroyed. Starch cannot turn it black if the helical shape is destroyed.  Saliva has an enzyme, amylase, that breaks down amylose.  Digestion of food begins in our mouth.*

Based on these questions, have the students write a suitable objective and hypothesis.  Some examples are given.

Results:

| | Chewed Bread | | | Bread + Saliva 30 minutes | |
|---|---|---|---|---|---|
| 30 seconds | 1 minute | Several minutes | Un-chewed Bread | Refrigerated | Not Refrigerated |
| | | | | | |
| | | | | | |
| | | | | | |
| | | | | | |

Conclusions:

*Overall, the chewed bread was less black when iodine was added than the unchewed bread.*

*The refrigerated bread and the chewed bread were the same.*

*All of the pieces of bread looked the same. I could see no difference.*

Have the students record their observations in the Results section. They should observe a decrease in the black color of the starch with the bread that has been chewed for longer time. Also, the refrigerated bread should be more black than the unrefrigerated bread.

Have the students write valid conclusions based on the data they have collected. Some examples are given.

Summarize the data and discuss with the students what is likely to have occurred:

1. The chewed bread and the bread with saliva at room temperature showed a decrease in the black color after iodine was added.
2. We know that bread contains starch (amylose).
3. We know that saliva has protein machines in it that begin the digestion of the food.
4. It is likely that the saliva contains a protein machine that breaks down the amylose in bread because of the color change with iodine.

These four statements are based both on data that has actually been collected (1) and information that has been gathered by other sources (2 and 3). The conclusion (4) is a likely conclusion, and most probably correct, but further data would need to be collected to prove that the concluding statement is true. Discuss how this investigation could lead to other experiments to prove the conclusion (i.e., a protein analysis to determine which proteins are in saliva). This is how real science works. Initial observations lead to additional experiments, which hopefully yield enough data to prove or disprove a given statement. Sometimes it takes years to collect all of the data, and sometimes enough data is never gathered. In these cases, the hypothesis remains unproven, and the most valid conclusions are only likely ones.

Review

Define the following terms:

protein    *A polymer of amino acids.*

amino acid    *A molecule that forms one unit of a protein chain.*

peptide bond  *The chemical link between amino acids in a protein.*

kinesin    *A protein that walks along a molecular road and carries a cargo.*

DNA    *A polymer of nucleotides.*

nucleotide  *A molecule that forms one unit in a DNA chain.*

double helix  *Two strands of DNA polymers wrapped around each other.*

DNA polymerase  *The protein machine that adds new nucleotides to a DNA chain.*

Draw a picture of kinesin.

What are the four bases that make up DNA?
*Adenine, Thymine, Cytosine, and Guanine.*

What are the symbols for the four bases that make up DNA?
*A, T, C, and G.*

NOTES:

# NOTES

# NOTES

# NOTES

# NOTES

# NOTES

# NOTES